Just A Stranger

Just A Stranger

(are you strong enough)

Scott Lance

Writers Club Press

San Jose New York Lincoln Shanghai

Just A Stranger
(are you strong enough)

All Rights Reserved © 2001 by Scott Lance Baumgardt

Writers Club Press
an imprint of iUniverse.com, Inc.

For information address:
iUniverse.com, Inc.
5220 S 16th, Ste. 200
Lincoln, NE 68512
www.iuniverse.com

ISBN: 0-595-19583-0

Printed in the United States of America

Sandy Jean   Marion Rose
Oprah Winfrey

PREFACE

Once upon a time a child was brought into this world of arrogance, hatred, jealousy, and dual personalities. This child catered to others around, following their examples and playing out their games. The people enjoyed this child's companionship, laughter, mistakes, and conquests. They could not let go.

One day this child was charged for a crime no one committed. The people around him bowed their heads, some with prayer and others with shame. How could this child do such a thing? Have we not taught him right from wrong. While others praised his strength, endurance, and the way this child still kept on giving, even to those who shamed his actions.

Trials and tribulations followed with this child meeting, if not exceeding, all the courts demands. Still, no innocence would be granted. "Have I done so wrong that I must live the rest of my life scarred, scared, and unwanted? Does the court know exactly what the original charge even is?" this child would ask often and pray more.

A child becoming an adult faced with responsibility and proof. Can you prove how you feel each day and where the feeling comes from? This child followed only the people in his life and yet they say their own records are 'clean'. This child has found support in his mother and a family he met along the way. Some of the people still argue about his innocence and betrayal, "Why didn't he ever listen to me?" But this is the world of jealousy, arrogance, pride, cruelty, and control.

This child has moved in a new direction. This child now makes choices of his own instead of listening to others - he has choices and tries to make them work. He shares dreams, designs, and writings instead of rumors, drinks, and sex. Most importantly he smiles not only on the outside but from the inside as well. He has grown.

I hope to see you in the next few chapters, but choose your role carefully for you are always being watched. May you trust in the mirror and love yourself for everyone else's benefit—we all need a laugh.

Warning: In these pages lay written mterial associated with drugs and alcohol. If you are not strong enough to deal with this kind of material substitute it with your own addiction, be it over-eating, spreading rumors, playing video games, or an obsession with the remote control. Feel free to be yourself.

WHAT ABOUT US 1

Phone rings four times, answering machine activates, and the person on the other end gets insecure.

"Who else is gonna answer the damn thing? I live alone," such is the life for Pat, a brown-eyed beauty with all the makings of a Hollywood starlet.

"Maybe it's just fate they hung up with no message and my caller I.D. didn't get the right signal to pick up their phone number." She had woke up from a Friday night stupor, phone rings—no one there, and she remembers the so-called meeting she was invited to by an old friend of hers. Why, was it fate? The yellow sticky note next to the phone with meeting arrangements. Her excuse was to be out of town. Phone rings and drags my ass over to the message and reminds me of the guilt I'm gonna feel if I don't show up......this time.

"Well, what are friends for, if not to get you out of the house to mingle and spill your guts about some romantic affair, an upcoming wedding, or a new career? Frankly, I don't care and thereto is why my friends are worried. Yes, just plain worried. I know this is the day of my reckoning. Straighten up Pat, you're talents are going to waste. Somebody out there is waiting for you." All this crap going through her head while motivating with a cup of nice black coffee and a Marlboro. Too bad she ran out of weed the night before.

One, two, three rings. "Okay, okay already!" this time she was picking up the receiver and catching whoever it was.

"Hello, this is Pat, I am alive..."

"Just your mother, dear. Is everything fine? Can you make it to your cousins wedding next month?"

"Yeah, right, next month. Who says if I'll make it that far?" Here she was wondering if one of today's topics would be covering weddings and she's holding the envelope.

"Well, if you're doing fine, you should be around for awhile. Did you go out last night and meet anyone?" Such a sincere woman was her mother. All things beautiful, all things right in her world, just made Pat wonder how deep that closet was. No one gets by with a little guilt and misfortune.

"Yes, I went out last night and got laid by some Sumo wrestler who is here visiting his Irish parents."

"Can I meet him?" Isn't this the way to tame a lion, rather a lioness, hit them back with whatever they're delivering.

"Don't go there, I am not in the mood for a slap-dance (a little quarrel cliché' she has shared with her mother over the years, argument is too strong of a word and people label you as having problems—who needs it?).

"You're never in the mood. But, just think about the wedding. I would like to have someone to talk to while I'm there and you're always my first thought."

"Thank you, I'll call you back before it gets near. But, I have to get ready for a reunion today."

"A reunion?"

"Just some friends I haven't seen for awhile. I'm sort of nervous about the whole thing, but I am going."

"Be careful. You know I love you and I'll be waiting for you to call me back. Okay?"

"Okay. I love you, too."

"Good-bye."

"Good-bye." As she hung up the phone the clock struck eleven bells.

"The note says 11:30 a.m., I am on my way." A quick look in the mirror and a little brush work through her long hair, her psyche built up, and she was out the door.

One thing with small towns is you can leave late and still make it early. The town she has been living in since day one, Mayville, Minnesota, population of 734 scattered soulsi, mostly living in the rural plains. You could see for miles in this flat, windy, and dry atmosphere, but it was home. All of it.

Living on the outskirts of this village she amused herself about being cultural, "I'm both country girl and city girl." The townspeople loved and adored her. Working as a secretary in the local attorney's office, J.J. & Blake, since graduating from high school in the mid-eighties, respect is the one thing she always took for granted.

2

Walking down the barren street on Second and Vine she pulled her memory back to the last time she had a visit with her buddies, the ones coming to town, the ones she admired, yet felt uncomfortable around.

Were they both coming or did one of them get married on the way here? She was hoping they would both show, making herself a little more scarce. This girl is one girl who would admit, "My business is my business, no matter who you are."

Kim, Becky, and Pat were never apart in high school, nonetheless in grade school. They were not related, which in itself is pretty weird in such a small town. They all came from broken families, divorced parents. On certain weekends either Kim or Becky would be gone visiting, saying 'hi' to the relatives on the other side of the fence. Pat was always a constant, unless her mom came up with a spur-of-the-moment vacation.

When they were together it was good times, smiles, and laughter. Kim stayed in town with her two brothers and her dad. Becky stayed with her mom and her grandma in a quaint little shack on Montgomery Street. Then there was Pat, who lived with her mom, although most people thought she was living on her own. Her dad called once in awhile, just to save face and remind her what she was missing out on. Even though there was nothing to miss out on.

Her mom was a working lady, cleaning houses to pay the rent. Yes, she had a few relationships over the years, but who would blame her. Being from a small town there is only so few men going around and it seemed every one of them was interested in this lady. Well, her daughter did not want to grow up in those shoes, she wanted her wide-open spaces and Cadillacs.

Once again, pacing herself down Second Avenue. "Going to meet some friends, talk smart and sassy. Hopefully they just want to get drunk and hang out away from everything. Isn't that what weekends are for?

Walking onto the lot of 'Serby's', the only bar in town, it's getting close to meeting time. "I'm here, where are my memory keepers?"

As she neared the side door leading into Serby's a car turned off Main Street and into the parking lot. It was a nice car, nothing too fancy or bright. Inside the car she noticed two heads, two smiles, and in her heart she knew there would be some laughter this afternoon.

"Hey, lady!" came the cry from the far side of the vehicle. Kim had been driving this maroon-on-maroon piece of art. Pat was getting geared up with sarcasm and mischief. The girls all knew who the trouble-maker was, they just didn't know why Pat never took it to Hollywood.

"So, then, how's the city girls?" Pat knew she sounded a bit uncomfortable, but the coffee hadn't kicked in and her mouth was dry, her head a little groggy, it was Saturday morning. It would be a short time from now until her feet were back in the swing of things. The bar was open and the door to it stood in reaching distance.

"We're just fine, Patricia," the ladies were singing in unison and they both knew how Pat just hated that name. "It was a long drive, about 2 hours, but we survived and we have decided to stay the night!"

"Oh, you just decide these things with no one's permission? Do you think you're good or just wanted?"

"Both," Becky was the one with all the answers. She didn't know it, everyone else did. Straight A student, never had to study, always breaking curfew, as if she ever had one. The girl was a role model for all those who wanted to be a success without leaving the couch.

All three of them skipped out on sports. Back in the 80's not much was in it for women and who wanted to be watching a ball when you could be watching, and mingling with, the spectators.

These girls did go out for all the Drama, one-act and three-act plays. If they were going to be on stage at least they could be holding onto somebody or kissing the best guy in the whole damn school. They wanted attention, they knew how to get it.

"How about it, we all thirsty?" Pat was getting impatient and the other two seemed as if a little chit-chat had been waiting. "I haven't had my wake-up, yet, and I'm thirsty."

The girls noticed Pat's abruptness, "Well, we figured on getting something to eat, first. Maybe across the street?" Kim pointed and gazed to the south, "Or is the old diner closed up like everything else in this town?" Kim knew the truth about this town, she had planned to stay after high school, but the same-old just quit working for her.

3

"No, the place is still serving three meals a day. You sure you want to eat?" Pat spoke like a teenager being told about visiting plans to her third cousins, even though she had been in her thirties for a few years.

"Sorry, but, we haven't had breakfast, yet" Kim pointed with her index finger to open mouth. "Does that answer your question?"

"Let's start walking," Pat was in no mood more confrontation.

"It is right across the street," Kim confirmed. "What's the matter with you, up all night?"

:You know where you can go with that comment. I was not up all night, just a little past three. There was a stranger in town and I had to show him around." This girl knew all the right buttons in all the right games, but did the city girls buy into it? Not a chance.

"We're all strangers in this town, crazy." The reply said it all, only Pat hadn't noticed it and the world didn't care if she did or not. Who's going to keep on waiting for someone who doesn't want to grow up, or should I say, wake up?

"Lovely, Irv's. Remember the nights? Remember the days?" Becky started to reminisce.

"Yeah, yeah, let's get inside and order." Pat's impatience remained noticeable. "I told you guys where my mind set is and I want to clear it up."

"Tequila!! Will that be shooters or Margaritas, ladies?" Becky had done a few nights work behind the bar.

"Now, now, leave little Patricia alone. We will play her game after we eat. And remember Pat, once we start, it's going to be Monday." Kim put out a warning.

"Thought you were leaving in the morning?"

"As if we're THAT responsible. Did you think we grew up or something?" Kim was getting back into this town. It was a matter-of-circumstance leading her out Mayville. College degree and a career in modeling, she had to accept the reward, but found the list long. Having her rendezvous with fame-in-the-city, she decided to stay in St. Paul, the other city, even when her modeling came to a stop. The thought of returning to Mayville surfaced often.

"Now you're speaking my language." Pat comforting with the strangers. They were becoming friends all over again.

"Our language," in a smirk tone, spoken by the ever-button-of-cute, Becky. "You didn't learn the fun and games side of life all by your little self, now, did you?"

"One for the fly!"

"All for the fly!" Spoken in unison as if they had never parted and were still practicing, on a daily basis, the good old hurrah, hurrah cheers of 1985.

Would Mayville be ready for the band to be back together? It might be only a one night gig, it could be the weekend. This town was always ready, they've been waiting. These girls, ladies in their true prime, belonged to this town with wide-open arms and smiles. The true essence of the "Greatest Show On Earth".

The bells chimed as the door opened. Irv, himself, had passed away one and one half years earlier, but the new owners had decided to keep his name. A memory thing or maybe just cheap advertisement.

"Let's get a window table," Becky always eager to be looking around.

"If you hadn't noticed, Becky, we are the only ones in here."

"And how may I treat you today, we usually close at noon on Saturdays, but I think we have an exception." A short guy with a mustache, sporting an apron of red and white checkers, approached the trio.

"Seems harmless to me," Becky whispered to Kim.

"Choose your table, the menus are in the centerpiece, and I'll be back to take your order." A polite man with a smile, a look of Minnesota.

"Out of the clouds, Becky," Pat could still sense when Becky was thinking. She could also sense some small-town judging. "By the way, Jack, there, he's from Iowa."

"Gag me."

"Gag you I shall do." Pat reached over and put her hands around Becky's neck.

"Okay, ladies, no violence. Let's eat and enjoy the day. We came miles to see our buddy, visit the patrons of our town, and who knows?" Kim raised her eyebrows.

4

"Who knows?" Pat picked up the vibe of meeting strangers in this small neck of the prairie. "Look out the window, you see anyone out there?"

"I will!" Here came Becky and chances were she would see someone, the girl just knew things.

"Pick up your menu," Pat demanded, "start looking, we're burning daylight."

"Daylight?" Kim snapped across the table. "Pat, since when do you worry about daylight?"

"Here we go again. All right, already, I don't worry about daylight. Let's just order and start having some fun."

"I already am." Sure enough, Becky spotted someone. Blue jeans, white T-shirt, Jean jacket draped over his shoulder, worn boots on his feet, and a white feather sticking up from the side of his hat. In return, he noticed her. "Told you I would find someone."

"Get out of the window. The guy's name is Bobby, lives about three blocks northwest of here."

"Now we're supposed to know directions?" Kim asked.

"Forget it. Just get out of the window. That guy keeps trying to hit on me in broad daylight."

"And you never took him up on anything? Or is it the daylight thing?" Kim needled.

"No! It has nothing to do with daylight," Pat did not want the attention.

"Pat you have changed. A guy hits on you and you leave him hanging?" Kim kept on.

"Well, Kimberly," Pat had enough, "maybe I've settled on one man." Surprised faces came across the table from Becky and Kim. The girl who stayed home grew up first?

"Who might this guy be?" Curiosity had hit a high note, especially with Kim. "Did you meet him lately, or has the little princess of Mayville been hiding something?"

"You're not jealous, are you?" Pat struck a chord. Her sarcasm went too far and the afternoon could be in jeopardy. One for all and all for one. They never kept secrets, no matter how far and how long it had been between visits.

"No, I'm not jealous. I'm just wondering if you're growing apart from us." Kim started getting sentimental, unbelievable.

"Ladies, have you decided on your meal?" Although Jack had admitted to breaking the rules on staying open past noon, he did have a life and wanted to cut out as soon as possible. Unless, the afternoon took a mysterious route and the ladies, in which he was feasting his eyes upon, asked him to join them.

"Yes, we're ready. Three hamburger baskets."

"Hold on, Pat. Maybe we want to order something else."

"Well, what will it be then?" Pat knew it would come back, and sure enough.

"I'll have a burger basket," replied Becky.

"Make it three," Kim was not going out-of-bounds, and she knew the other two knew what she wanted. Something simple, something quick.

"Three burger baskets. I will have them out in no time," Jack knew these girls belonged in a different league than the Division III club he was in. Make them the food, no small talk, and close shop before anyone else noticed the place was open.

"Now, Pat, as you were saying. Something about a man in your life?" Becky wasn't going to let some waiter interfere with this one. No one's off the hook when this big of a fish is at stake.

"And what if I told you it was Bobby?"

"The guy outside the window?" Kim sat stuped, but only for a moment.

"Okay, so you're messing with our heads," Becky and Kim realized it at the same time, but Becky was the only one to voice it.

"See, Kim, I haven't changed. I like throwing sticks into people's spokes just like before. When people start making accusations, I throw them a curve."

"I should have known," Kim nodded her head and shook her index finger at Pat.

"But as serious as you got, you're not thinking about getting old, are you?" Pat switched the hot seat. She could either get the answers out of Kim or she could drop the whole topic and get on with new business.

"I call it middle-aged crazy, but I am sticking to my guns."

"Good girl," Pat was leaving this one alone, for both their sakes.

"Bad girl," Becky butted in. "We all know bad girls live longer lives."

"And more of them!" Pat woke up. Her spirits were lifting and the shining was happening.

"Ladies, three burger baskets and I brought you some sodas. I hope you like Pepsi?"

5

"Thanks, Jack, anyone tell you how sweet you are?" Becky could not resist, she thought the guy was lonely and wide-open for a tease.

"My mother used to tell me that."

"Ohhhh!" The three ladies in front of him gave Jack the most sincere of glances while getting the hook set.

"Are you ladies staying around here long? I mean I know you," he glanced at Pat, "but how about you two?" Jack bit and the bait was set.

"Let's be real. Why would we want to stay around here when there's no men to be seen?" Punch number one.

"I could show you around." Jack didn't let up.

"Could you get us some more sodas, or something?" Kim hit push-happy on her mood ring. She did not want this guy around.

"Do you need more sodas?'

"No, we just thought you had better things to do."

"All of you thought that?"

"We're sort of a package deal. We know what each of us wants. So, if you don't mind." Kim had an eerie feeling about this guy. She knew how to play games, but she also knew some people didn't appreciate them being played.

"Well, the sooner you eat up, the sooner I can close up." Jack turned his back and walked. He knew he had to write out the bill, and how he felt like putting on some extra charges. Bitches.

"Boy, he sure got rude," nice little Becky. "You can tell he's not from Minnesota.

The ladies ate their burgers, finished their fries, and Jack put the bill on their table. No extra charges, no more small talk. He had better things to do, maybe get out of town and visit some friends in Iowa.

"Just leave the money on the table, I'll be in the back room cleaning up for the day." Jack stood by his motto 'the customer always comes first'. "I trust you girls."

"Thank you, hope you have a nice day." Pat did have to come back in here. Although, she had only been in here a few times in the last couple of months, she never knew when the next time would be.

"Do you think that guy has any family around here?" Becky continued with her curiosity.

"Why don't you ask?'

"Just leave it alone. Come on finish it up, Becky, and let's get across the street." Pat did not want to be wasting her batteries in a restaurant.

"Here, I'll get the tab." Becky paid for the meal by laying down a twenty and a five dollar bill. "This will cover it, he was a sweet guy."

"Man, are you desperate or what?" Pat couldn't believe the gratuity she was leaving behind. "This guy is going to follow us all over."

"So?"

"Let's go, Cinderella." Pat and Kim both put the 'claw' to Becky's neck and escorted her out. With a lunch to satisfy their appetite, the ladies were ready for adventure. The size of the town never mattered, boring was a word never used and the day had just begun.

"Hee-Haw! Country music is my life. Can't you listen to anything better than this?" And with that said, Tuck reached over and turned the knob, looking for a little up-beat instead of down-trodden.

"Hey, you messin' with my knob?" Simon slapped Tuck's hand. "Do I mess with your knob?"

"Come on, I only want to get **up** for work," Tuck explained.

"Okay, just because," Simon gave in, "you're giving me free orange juice at the bar."

Tuck held up his hands, "No problem, orange juice it is. Now, can I have the knob?"

"Turn it, dude. This song is a little on the somber side."

Tuck gazed, "A little? Here we go, station K.S.A.M.," Tuck tweaked in the frequency. "Now I can relate. I mean my life's not all bad."

"Except for the DWI hanging over your head," Simon reminded.

"Had to bring it up, didn't you?" Tuck cringed and backhanded Simon in the forehead. "I have my stipulations and I can follow their directions."

"No alcohol for one year, possible treatment, and AA meetings," Simon continued.

"Hey, I know the rules. Besides, I'll just go with you to those meetings." Tuck gave a pleasing glance, putting Simon on the receiving end.

"You have me, there. "Simon went through the same obstacle a year and some earlier, DWI and loss of license. "I guess I could go back to those meetings, they never hurt me." Once Simon finished all his requirements, including re-testing and treatment, he pocketed his license and shelved going to AA.

"They still have the meetings on Monday nights?"

"Yep, that's what the court papers say. Monday and Thursday nights at the church basement in Hontra or Saturday mornings at some guys house," Tuck tried to remember his options.

"And you didn't go this morning?"

"Ah!" Tuck reached over and cranked the volume. "When's the last time you want?"

Simon shrugged his shoulders in guilt, "I'll go with ya."

"Cool. Thanks, Bud." Tuck punched Simon's shoulder, sat back with a grin, and opened his window all the way, so he could stick his head out.

"Man, dude, you are a dog!"

"Just combing my hair!"

Tuck and Simon, two castaways from far away places. Tuck moved in from a northern city, while Simon took 35W up from Kansas and hooked a left. They now shared a farm place about seven miles south of Mayville. It was only by coincidence they both moved here at the same time, October 19, 1998.

Simon had a sister going to the University of Minnesota, but after one week luck struck him as he ran into a couple of Engineering majors, telling him about a production plant in southern Minnesota, specializing in truck accessories. Next thing you know Simon found himself working in Hontra and living on a farm place south of Mayville.

Tuck's story started up in St. Cloud, but from there the story melts together with Simon's. Until a couple of weeks ago when Tuck got pulled over on the way back from Hontra. Working the second shift, going out with a few co-workers after a busy week, Friday night and the crowd is up, slamming a bit too much 'Captain' and 'Maui', 1:45 a.m. on the police report is all I need to say. Tuck found himself between a rock and a hard place, never one to let his family help him out of a crisis. It had been ten years since he had last heard about his dad.

Tuck worked second shift, Simon somehow managed to get on first shift. So much for getting a ride to work, and he was not going to ask his co-workers for any hand-outs or pencil in a one-way walk of twenty miles each day on his schedule. He got himself in this mess, it was up to him to get himself out of it. So, the first Monday, after the incident happened, he walks in to Serby's, the only bar in Mayville, sits down for a tap of Bud and asks for a job. The next words he hears are "you can start tomorrow."

Being on the late side, Simon pushed the petal down, "Shit, you're gonna be late!"

"It's a bar job, there's no such thing as being late," Tuck wore a mischievous grin. "By the way, Tonto, what are you doing today?"

"Cruise out to the lake and watch the ice melt away."

7

"What!?"

Simon turned the volume down, "I said, go out to the lake. Supposed to get real nice out."

"And I'm stuck inside. Shit!" Tuck lightly punched the dash.

While these two were rushing to get to Serby's, Mike Serby, the owner himself, paced the floor, "He's worked here two Saturdays and been late both of 'em. Here I am, supposed to be going to a wedding up in Minneapolis and this kid is yanking my chain, pulling on the nerve strings."

"Too much coffee, there, pal?" Burt, the local mechanic, gestured.

"Yeah, maybe, but still the kid should be here."

"Give him time. He's a good kid," albeit Tuck was nearing 35, he just looked like 25, and Burt was only a few years older. The way Burt seen it, he didn't know if Mike had the same understanding, anybody younger than himself was a kid.

Simon pulled into the alley behind Serby's and Tuck got out of the truck. Tuck ran around the back end of the vehicle and into the bar. There's a small room in the back and Tuck tried making it look as if he had been there for awhile. Too bad Mike Serby had walked into this space a few minutes earlier and remained standing by the doorway.

"Hey, Tuck. Out of breath?" Serby stood with hands on hips.

"Uh, yeah." Tuck stopped in his tracks, rather speechless, and tried catching his breath.

"No problem, it is a bar job, right?" Serby was not in a good mood. "I'll be back early tonight to check on you. This staying open late thing has got to stop." Mike Serby exited out the back.

How did he know about the late nights and 'just a bar job' thing?" Tuck asked himself, light from loss of oxygen. "Man, is that guy watching me?"

Tuck tried shaking it off and walked into the bar area, one customer, Burt. "How's it going?"

"Uh, you talkin' to me?" Burt replied.

"Yeah, I guess. How's it going?" Tuck tried again for proper response.

"Not bad, but I sure could go for a football game." Burt played full-back for Mayville High School and then moved on to a community college in northern Minnesota for two years. Mayville joined two other schools over the past ten years because of student numbers and high costs of education, while Burt split the community college, because, in his terms, he knew enough. He has been the only mechanic in Mayville for the last seven years.

"Football in March. Don't think it'll be on cable today."

"Let's go outside, then. You and me, one on one."

"Are you gay? I'm not playing against you." Tuck gave a bewildered look.

"Then fill up my glass," Burt held his mug in the air. "Bud Light."

Simon parked his truck in the back alley and walked around to the front of the bar. Opening the door, he swaggered in.

"There's your man, Burt. He'll play some ball," it was Tuck's job to get the customers involved.

"What?" Simon stood aback.

Burt stood up from his bar stool, "Come on!" Burt got down in a three-point stance and started to holler, "Hut, hut, one, two, hut!" and released himself from the floor, darting towards Simon.

Simon caught the clues, stood his ground, and as Burt smacked him above the waist, went flying six feet back, almost right back out the door.

"What the hell you doing?" Tuck yelled.

Burt reached down and helped Simon to his feet, "you all right, little buddy?"

"No problem," Simon confirmed, wiping off his pants. "Say, Tuck, you have my O.J.?"

Tuck stood amazed, Burt had leveled him and he just got right back up, "Sure thing, Simon. Is this the stuff makin' you ...numb?" Tuck didn't think Simon was tough or strong, he had to be numb.

"No. Orange juice keeps my hair shinin'." Simon brushed his right hand through his strawberry blonde.

"Want me to hit him, again?" Burt didn't like sarcasm and his face showed it.

"Settle down," Simon patted Burt on the shoulder, "I'm serious."

"Yeah," Burt was always on the wire about liking this Simon character, he just couldn't understand him. "Say, if he's not payin' for the juice why am I payin' for the brew?"

"Simon, see what you start?" Tuck gave a cross look at Simon. "Tell you what, Burt, one on the house, but that's it. And don't go running to Serby."

8

"Hey, you're the only beertender in this town. Why would I wanna rat on ya?"

"Well, since you already paid for that one," Tuck had taken the money off the bar while Burt was putting a 'stick' on Simon, "I'll give you the next one when you're ready."

Burt gave a cold stare to his mug, eyed Tuck, "Time me."

"What?" Tuck wasn't aware of drinking games played out at some northern college.

"Time the slam," Burt picked up his mug and nodded an agreement

"Okay, got ya," Tuck caught on. "You ready? And go!"

Burt put the mug to his lips, opened up and poured. Having emptied the contents he set the mug back down, "Slam!"

"Three and one half seconds."

"What kind of time you keeping?" Burt sat displeased.

"One thousand one, one thousand two," Tuck confirmed.

"Ah, shit. Give me my free one." Burt slid his mug over to Tuck. "Were you counting?" Burt nudged Simon.

"What? I wasn't paying attention," Simon blinked himself back from a faraway place.

"Never mind." Burt turned back to Tuck, topping off his mug with a nice head, and Pfffft! Beer went splashing and sputtering.

"Damn, I hate this shit. You just never know when the kegs goin' dry," Tuck jumped out of the way just in time from getting soaked, letting go of the handle, and standing disgruntled.

"Ha, ha," Burt laughed at Tuck's misfortune, "almost got ya!"

"But it didn't, and you get to wait," all's even in love and war.

"How 'bout the other tapper?" Burt questioned as if someone stole his football.

"You laugh, you wait." Tuck made his point clear and left the bar, going down the rickety stairs to change the line off the empty keg and attaching it to a full keg.

Tuck had heard another customer enter the bar, but proceeded to change kegs. Burt and Simon turned around, hearing the door open and the footsteps on the wooden floor, "Magic Man!" Simon greeted.

"What's happening!" Irvin, nicknamed 'Magic' because of his moves on and off the court, placed a burp right behind his own greeting. "Is there a bartender in this place?"

"Changin' kegs," Burt still looked sympathetic.

"Well, give me some whiskey. Don't need no beer to keep me happy!" Irvin displayed a smile of shine.

Tuck breezed up the stairs and took his position behind the bar, "Magic. What's up?"

"Drinks on me! I gotta good feelin' about today."

"Drinks on you?" Burt lit up, almost stuttering, "In that case, pour me some Jack."

"You, son-of-a-bitch," Tuck had ran down to switch kegs and now the bastards didn't want beer.

"Hey, the guys buying," Burt slipped a half-ass apology. "What would you do?"

Tuck nodded his head, keeping his thoughts to himself. "Okay, so you want a Jack/Coke, Irvin, Captain/Coke? and Simon another O.J.?"

"Hey, I'm not buying no orange juice. You go get that at the grocery store," Irvin pushed in.

"Fine with me," Simon didn't mind Irvin's attitude, "I'll get my own."

"I don't know about you, Simon," Irvin sneered. "I'm buying him a Tequila Shooter," Irvin demanded while pointing at Simon.

"Fine with me," Simon nodded towards Tuck. "It's his money."

Something about Simon bothered Irvin. Was it the light red hair, the goody-goody attitude, the orange juice, or was it the fact he moved here from Kansas?

Irvin's smile now resembled a snarl, "Give me some quarters, too, while you're at it."

"No problem," Tuck finished mixing the Captain and the Jack, and slid Simon the Shooter. He took the money from Irvin and made change. "Here you go, and three dollars worth of quarters. Now play somethin' decent." Tuck remembered the music Irvin picked out the last time he was in here.

"Ah, what's wrong with a little 'Fishin' in the Dark'?" Irvin put his smile back on, eased his shoulders back, saluted, and did a right toe to left heel 180.

"What was that all about?" Burt asked.

9

"Ah, he misses boot camp," Tuck remarked. Maybe the reason behind Tuck and Irvin's camaraderie was the fact they shared military stories. Tuck was in the Air Force, while Irvin did a small stint in the Marines.

"Do you Irvin?" Burt asked stupidly.

"Just drink your sauce," Irvin turned back to deliver his remark and then continued to proceed towards the juke box.

Burt, Tuck, and Simon got a good laugh out of the short exchange, knowing the reason behind Irvin's short-lived Marine life. Getting busted with another guy's dope.

Irvin plugged in four quarters, saving a few for the computer games, and started pushing memorized buttons, 1434, 2207, 1777. He stopped after his three favorites and looked for some new stuff. Noticing nothing new, he stepped back and looked out the window besides the juke box. "Hey, Tuck, who's Grand-Am?"

"Got me, I hadn't noticed."

"Aren't you paying attention? It's sitting in your parking lot?" Irvin put his eyes back to the car and tried registering it with his memory bank. "I wonder if it's someone I know."

Burt stood up and sauntered over to Irvin, "Must've came in after I got here."

"When was that? Nine o' clock?"

"No. I got here about eleven."

"Tuck, you know if Pat had anybody come visit?" Irvin had been waiting for the return of Kim and Becky ever since they left, two years ago. Irvin spent a night with Kim and he was always wondering if he would get his chance with Becky.

"She didn't say anything."

"Hmm, I just have a feeling," Irvin repeated. "Where could they be?"

"I don't know," Burt gave his answer and went back to his stool.

Simon finished up the last of his ice cubes and handed his Shooter over to Burt, "See you guys."

"Hey, thanks," Burt accepted the Shooter. "See you around."

Tuck turned the music up, Irvin picked out the remaining selections, and Burt inspected the Rox glass in his hand. Simon laid down some small change and headed out the back door.

"Where's he going?" Irvin asked, pointing at Simon's back. Simon heard him but kept on walking.

"Cruisin' out to the lake," Tuck answered.

"I don't know what it is about him," Irvin took a stool.

"Hey, he treats me good," Burt held up the Shooter.

"That son-of-a, man I'm gonna get him next time. Here, fill me up another." Irvin handed his glass to Tuck.

"What is it? Just because he don't drink?" Tuck interrogated.

"I don't know. He just gives me an eerie feeling," Irvin shivered.

"Well, for your information, I can't drink, neither," Tuck implied, handing the glass of Captain back to Irvin.

"Oh, so you going sissy, too?" Irvin's judgment came out.

"No, asshole, court-ordered," customer or not, Irvin deserved the comment.

"Oh, like you couldn't afford a lawyer?" Irvin's arrogance was shining through.

Tuck kept his cool by biting his lip, and then offered a little advice, "Just remember I'm the bartender here today and since I don't own this place I can get you as messed up as I want. And then when you walk out that door I'll give you a seven minute headstart before I call in your license number."

"You would that?" Burt asked, getting a bit nervous, trying to recount what he had already consumed.

"What do you think, Irvin?" Tuck put a cold stare into Irvin's eyes. "Or should I call ya Magic?"

Irvin broke Tuck's glare by looking down, "Hey, I'm sorry man. Didn't mean to get personal."

Tuck regrouped as the beginning of song number 1777 started to play (insert your favorite) and grabbed his bar-rag, "Hey, now, this is a good tune."

Take a deep breath you will soon be given your signal, a cue, to intervene on the stage. Make your last second adjustments. Spotlights are in the distance, the seats are full, don't sweat, keep your cool, and there's your signal—action!

Head up, shoulders back, you approach center stage to confront your co-star. "Greetings, Mr. Withers." And nothing comes back. Do you follow with your next line, the planned script, or do you ad-lib, trying to correct your co-stars mistake. Life is but a play, do you know your part?

Simon hopped into his truck and drove out of the alley onto First Avenue, he was going to take a right, which would lead him out of town, but the truck took a left—'follow your instincts'. He approached Main Street taking another left, "Whoa! The girls are back in town," Simon noticed Kim, Pat, and the one he admired most, maybe because of his short one-niter with her, Becky. He acted as though he had just seen a rare species not known to exist in these parts. He could be right.

Simon drove up to the ladies, who had just crossed the street, coming to a stop on the wrong side of the road, "Hey, ladies, what's up?"

"Hi, Simon," Pat returned. "You remember these two, don't you?"

"Oh, yeah. How's it going Becky?" Simon didn't hide his admiration.

"I'm doing good, and you?"

"Say, Simon?" Pat cut in to the greetings, she wanted to party, and walked up to Simon's window. "You have any smoke?"

"No," Simon wore a permanent smile, "but I know where to get some."

Pat turned to her guest, "Ready for some treats?" She put her index finger and thumb together, putting them up to her lips, and sucked in, raising her eyebrows.

"We're ready!" Becky spoke for the both of them. "Right, Kim?" and then followed with a cover-her-ass agreement.

Kim nodded her head. She would go along for the ride. It had been awhile since she had smoked anything, nonetheless take any kind of drugs, but these were friends and memories. She had to take advantage of the full glass.

"Well, you all want to hop in here?" Simon grinned as he patted his bench seat.

"No!" Becky responded, "I have more room in my car. Besides, since we're dishin' out treats I brought some of my own."

Simon realized the situation of him being used just to get some smoke for the ladies, but what's wrong with being seen with so much beauty. "I'll just park my truck and be right with ya."

The ladies breezed towards the car, and noticing the warm weather, shed their jackets revealing why one had been a model, one a surviving actress—short stints for commercials and a glamorous waitress in a strip club, and the other a self-proclaimed Miss Mayville. They opened the car doors, flinging their jackets in the backseat, and waited for Simon. "Come on, Howdy!"

Simon came running across the street. "We need anything to drink?"

"Not unless you do," Kim answered. "We have coolers in the trunk." She might not be into drugs, except for today, but she did like her wine coolers and Champagne.

"No, all's fine then. I quit drinking." Simon climbed into the backseat, where Pat joined him.

Becky took position behind the wheel and Kim took the navigation seat, "Just tell us where to go."

Becky turned the ignition, put her into reverse, and upon putting the transmission back into drive put a little force into the accelerator. "Time for us to fly!"

"Hey, did you guys hear some tires?" Irvin asked for assurance.

"No, I don't think I did," Burt sat in a daydream.

Irvin punched Burt in the shoulder, "Wake up! Man, I hope we didn't miss 'em." Irvin got up from his stool and walked back over to the window. "Shit! They're gone."

Tuck came from around the bar, "Did you see who it was?"

"No. I was sitting at the bar," Irvin pointed towards his stool, blaming it for his misfortune.

"So, you weren't paying attention?" Tuck liked get-backs. You accuse someone of doing something and you yourself are doing the same thing.

"Uh. You got me," Irvin accepted the tag. "Say, Pat has a cell phone. Do you know her number?"

11

"Yep, she gave it to me last night. Tuck pulled out his wallet and pulled out a piece of paper, "Here it is."

"Cool! I'll find this party." Irvin grabbed the piece of paper and jaunted over to the phone.

Tuck realized he had just lost a customer and the beginning of a long afternoon had started.

One ring, two ring, Pat heard something in her purse, "My phone's ringin'!" She grabbed it out of her purse and pushed the necessary button, "Hello!"

"Hey, Pat, this is Irvin," who had the face of a Cheshire cat.

"Guess where I'm at?" Pat didn't mind playing games with the opposite sex, either.

"I don't know, maybe in some maroon Grand-Am."

"You cheated!"

"Oh, well. I'm at Serby's," Irvin thought it best to state his location. "Where you guys headed?"

"Well, Simon said he could hook us up with some treats. Wanna come out?"

Irvin cringed at the announcement of Simon, "What you got him along for?"

"It doesn't matter, silly. Do you wanna come out?" Pat dodged her excuse for Simon, she just wanted to party.

"Where you headed?" Irvin had an idea, but he had been on wild-goose chases before.

"Pete and Dan's place, Cyprus Lake."

"Okay, well, I'll finish my drink and be out the door," Irvin's skin felt goosebumps on the inside as he hung up the phone.

"Who's the secret caller?" Kim asked with curiosity, having her own interests and strategies.

"Remember Irvin, Irvin Baker?" Pat replied.

"Yeah, the farm guy. He still have those cows?" Kim rather ask a stupid question then to admit her own desires for a guy she had slept with two years ago.

"Yeah, he still has cows," Pat answered with a touch of suspicion. "Is that all you want to know?"

Before Pat could ask her question, Kim had turned to Becky, "Say, pull over. Let's get some of those coolers out of the trunk."

"No problem, big sister." Becky parked off the side of the road and popped her trunk. "You want a cooler, Patricia?"

"Man, guys," Irvin jumped back to his stool elated, slapping Burt's back, "I have scored!"

"So, you leavin' us all alone?" Tuck showed the face of a homeless dog.

"Not my problem. You have the bar and I have cows. You get a paycheck and I get afternoons off." Irvin lifted his glass and emptied its contents. "Whew!"

"Well, at least you could mention us to the others," Tuck pointed to himself and then to Burt. "You know? Maybe all of ya could come back here."

"We'll see, bartender. I have some ladies to meet." Irvin stuck his chin up, smiled as if standing on the highest platform at a reward ceremony, and nodded his head, "See ya, boys!"

"Asshole," Tuck said, Burt thought it. The rest of the day seemed long away for the both of them.

Becky had jumped out of the car and returned with three wine coolers, "sure you don't want one, Simon?" asked with a cordial grin.

"Nope, I quit drinkin', but thanks anyway."

"Okay, you sure have changed," Becky remembered her last weekend in Mayville as well as Simon did. They both got pretty wasted and ended up skinny-dipping in Cyprus Lake.

"Well, after my DWI last year, I don't have much of a choice."

"That sucks," Becky handed a cooler to Pat and sat herself down. She then handed the other two bottles to Kim, "Can you open this for me?" Kim did as was asked while Becky shifted the car into drive.

"How much further?"

"You know," Pat confirmed. "On the north side of the lake, the old cabin spot."

"Okay, right up the road."

"Yeah, about five more miles and a right turn."

The temperature rose twenty degrees from this morning, the needle now coming upon 65 degrees. Being Minnesota, you could never quite predict the weather in March, or April for that matter. It could still be snowing, anyway the weather channel had forecasted it for this evening.

12

Becky came upon a T-road, with Cyprus Lake straight ahead. She took a left.

"Okay, first place on your left," Simon gave his unneeded second opinion.

"I remember. But thanks, anyway." They all used to come out here every weekend, the whole high school, party from Friday night until Sunday afternoon, and summers, that was a whole new story.

"Oh, yeah, that's right, you grew up here." Simon sat back in his seat thinking about his stupid remark.

"It's all right, Simon. You gonna go up to the door?" Pat backed him up.

"Yeah. I'm sure they'll be home," Simon had no problem being the runner, the middle-man, or whatever you called it, he just wondered where Pat had been getting her weed, otherwise. He also knew to keep his thoughts to himself.

Becky pulled in front of the unattached garage, which sat across the driveway from the remodeled cabin, "Okay, party time!" She got out of the car and let Simon out, "Want me to go with you?"

"No, it's all right. If their home I'll wave you on in." Simon walked up to the side door, or was it the front door, you couldn't really tell. He knocked three times and gave a finger-roll. The door opened.

"Hey,dude, how's it going?" Pete rolled his eyes until they were used to the sunlight. "Nice day, huh?"

"Say, you have any smoke?" Simon did not hesitate.

"Yeah, what you lookin' for?"

"Just hold on, it's not really for me," Simon didn't play a very good middle-man, but, then again, the girls he was with were hometown. "Pat, Becky, Kim come on up!"

"Oh, Simon got some chicks. Cool, dude," Pete grinned at the scenery coming forward.

"Isn't Donna with you?" Simon wanted Pete to stay true to his own lady. He knew Donna, rather went out with her, when he had first moved here from Kansas. Pete was about three years younger than Donna, but in this day and age, it didn't matter.

"Yeah, she's in the living room." Pete took a step back, while holding the door open, "Come on in." He didn't mean to be a gentleman he just wanted a good look as the ladies came walking by.

"Hi, Pete, long time," Pat greeted, not having seen Pete since the Christmas party.

"Yeah," Peter shrugged his shoulders and looked down sheepishly, sort of in a shy manner, but he kept looking. "So, who are your friends?"

"Becky, Kim, meet Pete. Can I assume Donna is home?" Pat would not leave her friends get mixed up with someone who's already involved. Right! It was more of a if-I -can't -have-him, neither-can-you.

"Yeah, Donna's home. Just go into the living room and I'll be in shortly. Say, Pat, what were you looking for?"

"A quarter."

"Sounds cool. I'll bring it in there," Pete usually kept his stash down the basement because no one else trusted the make-shift steps going down there. Once he got to the basement he pulled an old crock jar from beneath some benches, "she'll like this."

Simon was the first to enter the living room, "Hi, Donna."

"Hi, Simon," Donna straightened out the couch she had been laying on. "I was wondering whose car that was."

"Oh, it's not mine. You remember Kim and Becky?" Simon knew she remembered Becky, the cause of their own break-up.

"Yes, I think I do," Donna also figured it best to play dumb and forgetful. "Hi, Pat."

"Hi, Donna. You remember these girls?"

"Yeah, Simon just told me." Donna did not want any arguments, besides, her and Pete were doing better than just fine. In her thoughts, a proposal was right around the corner. "Why don't you all sit down," she motioned to the couch. "Anyone need a cold-one?"

The girls had left there wine coolers in the car, "Sure, I'll have one," Becky was the first to speak.

"Yeah, you can count me in," Pat came in second, followed by Kim, while Simon asked for a glass of water.

13

"Coming right up!" Donna went into the kitchen as Pete came up from the basement, "Hey, sweetheart, nice company."

"Well, uh, yeah," Pete hadn't yet figured out the female language. "I think so?"

"It's okay. Here have a beer," Donna handed him a can and stacked three into her one arm and held one in her other hand. She spent some time as a bartender, waitress, and on some unlucky occasions, a bouncer. Albeit, a very good looking bouncer.

Pete took the chair next to the kitchen doorway as Donna handed out the beers. She went back into the kitchen to get Simon's water when she heard a knock. Someone was at the door. "Pete, can you get the door? Ah, never mind. I'll get it," She answered herself before Pete got the whole question. Donna strolled over to the door and opened it, "Pete! It's your friend, Irvin!" The last name Pete wanted to hear.

Knock-out

The definition of obsession is the act of ruling over another person, object, or even a place.

If you were to let go of a best friend, could you stand on your own two feet, making decisions carried with consequences if mislead? Are you one to boldly go where no one has gone? Columbus, Norman Rockwell, and even Charlie Chaplin, had spirit.

So, when the mood starts swinging, can you stay in control?

"Here, Pat," Pete through her a quarter bag on his way to the door.

"Cool, have any papers?" Pat fondled the nicely wrapped baggie, opened it, and put her face into it. "Smells good."

Becky checked the contents of her purse, "Here, I found some. And guess what else I found?" a mischievous face.

"What else you find, Becky?" Simon leaned forward, still hanging onto a slight crush.

Becky lifted up a small 'butterfly', "Cocaine!"

Pete had paused when Pat asked about the papers, leaving Irvin wait outside the door, "Oh, man, powder. You girls come prepared."

"Excuse me?" Donna stood on the other side of Pete. "There's someone waiting for you."

"Oh, yeah. I was just saying," Pete knew it was no use trying to explain his personal euphoria.

"Never mind, Peter." Donna also understood his trouble with explanations.

Pete walked to the door, "What's up, neighbor?" Being Irvin lived just two miles down the road.

"I heard there's a party going on!" Irvin in his up-beat persona, which annoyed Pete.

"Who says?" No one told Pete about any party, and it was his house.

Irvin never one to blame the girls, but always willing to get Simon into trouble, "Simon told me."

"Simon? Just wait," Pete shut the door in Irvin's face and walked back into the living room. "Simon, front and center." Pete motioned Simon to follow him to the door. "Did you tell him I was having a party?"

Once again in the middle, hell Simon was born there, "Yep. I told him me and Pat were on our way out here with two city girls and that you would have no problem helping us share our dope. Isn't that right, Irvin?"

"Uh, yeah," Irvin stood a little caught-off-guard. "Can I come in?"

"Okay, but any funny business you and Simon have to leave." Pete layed the ground rules and went back into the living room. "You have one rolled, yet?"

"Yes," Pat held up a tightly wound joint. "But Becky needs something."

Pete looked over to Becky, "Oh, a mirror?"

"Here, let's smoke this first," Pat held Pete from leaving the room. "Anyone have a light?" She didn't smoke cigarettes, so, why would she be carrying a lighter.

"Here you go," Irvin pulled out a Bic from his pocket. He didn't smoke cigarettes, neither, but he always prepared himself for the unexpected.

"Thanks, Irvin," Pat took the lighter and sparked the joint. Inhaling deeply. She then passed it to Kim, ladies first, besides, she didn't want Irvin to get any ideas. She had been toying with him for about five years, but after he slept with Kim, her trust had to be built back up.

The joint was passed to all: Kim, Becky, Simon, Pete, Donna, Irvin, and back to Pat. "One more round and we'll have to twist another," Pat hinted. The room filled with laughter and a cough from Irvin.

"Holding to long, farm-boy!" Pete grinned towards Irvin.

Pat would be right, the joint made one more round and turned into a roach. Pete got up from his chair and turned on the stereo, Donna and

Kim were sharing giggles, Becky fiddled with the wrapped cocaine, looked at Simon then over to Donna and back to Simon, sat back in the couch and smiled at the ceiling. Pat and Irvin looked around the room and soon as the music came on started nodding their heads to the beat. "All right!" Pete felt it necessary to release.

Donna jumped, being Pete yelled right behind her. "Ohh!" she looked around with a snarl, which turned into a smile and a pinch behind Pete's knee, "You silly."

15

Simon noticed Becky looking back and forth, then settling on the ceiling, "What?" he asked Becky, giving her a nudge with his elbow.

"Huh? Oh, nothin'. I was just thinking." Becky had been out practically every night this week.

"Am I tired or just burnt out?" she wondered to herself.

Kim had now transferred the giggles to Pat as they both played with Irvin's mind, whispering to each other and then looking over to Irvin with smiles and question marks. Donna noticed the mind playing, and then noticed the empty hands in Irvin's lap.

"Irvin, need a beer?" Donna asked.

"Ha, I don't know. What are you two laughing at?" Irvin wanted to join the giggles, but not if it was on him.

"Nothing," Pat replied. "You know your flies open?"

Irvin quickly looked down, "Ah, is not."

Kim, Pat, Donna, and Pete nearly came to tears from laughing, "Another one on you, farm-boy!" Pete exclaimed as if in some kind of competition.

Simon didn't hear the punchline, but after seeing Irvin abruptly look down he figured who the joke was on, "Got him, again." He said to himself, snickering.

Becky came down from the ceiling and joined the laughter. She had no idea what it was all about, but the laughing felt good. She liked the feeling of letting go of all emotions, troubles, and worries. She had been out all week because she was covering up the fact her job was no longer needing her services and telling Kim would only add to Kim's worries.

Donna had to get up from her chair to stop laughing, "Oh, my goodness. I haven't laughed that hard for a long time. She went into the kitchen.

"Ha, are we done, yet?" Pat asked, wiping her face.

Kim sat back in relief and Becky noticed the piece of paper in her hand, "We still want some?"

"I don't know," Simon nodded his head in disapproval.

"Yes, I'll have some!" Pat acknowledged. "It's been awhile."

"And I know Kim rather not, right?" Becky asked to be sure, since she hardly seen Kim smoke dope, either.

"You are correct," Kim started giggling, again. "Man, I am high."

"I'll get you a mirror." Pete left the room and took the door off the medicine chest.

"Here, Irvin," Donna came back from the kitchen with a beer, holding it as though she were the welcoming committee to New York for every foreigner coming in via the east coast "Last one."

"You sure?" Irvin held the can, "it's your last one."

"We can always get more, and besides, I'm sure the others didn't come out here dry," she looked at Pat for assurance.

"Nope, we got more in the car," Pat just smiled.

Simon stood up from the couch, "I'm going outside for a bit."

"Women getting you all worked up, Simon?" Irvin asked boyishly.

Simon turned back to Irvin, "Matter-of-fact Magic, yes, they are." He then left the room and walked outside. Kim, not knowing why, got up from the couch and followed Simon.

"Where you going?" Pat wondered.

"Out here, I guess," Kim's eyes were but small slots as turned to answer Pat.

"You are stoned, girl!" Pat fell beck into the couch laughing. Kim smiled, turned back towards the small hallway, and continued on her way—outside.

Pete came back into the living room, noticing Kim heading out the door, "What's up with that?"

Becky looked up from her small square of powder, "She don't like you."

"What?" Pete didn't expect the comment.

"Just kidding," Becky smiled and held out her hand, "that for me?"

"Yeah, I know it works," Pete handed her the glass door, "and here's a razor blade, just in case."

Donna didn't sit to keen on the flirty exchange, but she knew how to handle Pete, "Say, honey," Pete turned towards Donna, "there's some straws in the kitchen." She just made him run little errands, but, then again, who was he really running errands for.

"So, Becky, how long you stayin'?" Irvin, the last guy in the room. Sure, he had figured Pat might be waiting for him to grow up, but what better way than to show her. Pat sat studyingly to

16

Irvin's every move. "I mean, last time you stayed a couple of days." Instruction number one has been followed, paying attention and remembering.

"I don't know," Becky succumbed, "it's more up to Kim than me." She continued chopping up her rocks into fine sand, white sand. "How many lines we need?"

"One, two," Pat counted by pointing out the participants, "five of 'em."

"And here's some straws," Pete laid down three plastic straws, the ones with the flexible rib, and sat directly back into his chair. "Hey, sweetie," he gave Donna a nice, reassuring smile and then lip-synched 'I love you'. Pete had too many good things going with his girl and no matter how hard one might try there was no way anyone would step in between them.

"Simon, wait for me!" Kim yelled from the top step to Simon, who had started walking down the path towards the lake. Simon stopped and turned around. "Just wait, I wanna grab a wine cooler!" Kim darted over to the car and popped the trunk. She grabbed a smooth bottle of Berry, slammed the trunk, and went running towards Simon.

"Okay, chop, chop, Donna want first dibs?" Becky asked, rather politely.

"Why, thank you, Becky," Donna accepted, bygones are bygones, and reached for the mirror.

Sunshine and druggin', the afternoon kicked in and the souls were being counted. The cabin dwellers and the sea merchants. The rock-n-rollers and the wind-listeners. Was there any difference?

Back in Mayville, Serby's door had opened to some bygone travelers and sun followers, mostly stopping in for a 12-pack of their favorite. Tuck and Burt took turns with the remote, shared some football knowledge, and were about to begin on a shelled peanut spree, while a couple from out of town, anyway Burt thought they were, sat over by the dart board. Sometimes just sitting and talking, sometimes actually playing a game of 301, but at least they kept the juke box going (insert your favorite 3 songs).

"Well, Burt, since you're done watching that show (insert your uncle's favorite rerun) it's my turn to run the clicker," Tuck spoke softly and then cradled the remote in his hand. "Unless, of course, you know of some football special."

"Nope," Burt nodded his head, "not today." He took a drink from his mug, put it down, and ran his finger along the rim.

"Hey! Don't be falling asleep on me." Tuck did not want to go the afternoon solo.

"I'm just thinkin'." Burt bent his neck upward, "you have anything going with Patty?"

"I gotta admit I've tried. Why?" Tuck set the remote down and grabbed a peanut.

"Well, I'm just tellin' ya, between you and me," Burt kept his hand lazily on the bar while pointing with his index finger, "she's already taken."

"By you?" Tuck hadn't realized, until now, Pat was seeing anyone. "I mean, if you're with her, well, then, I'm not." Tuck took a step back and lifted his arms in surrender mode.

"No, no," Burt winced. "Well, there was a time, but not now."

"You and Pat?"

"It's was more like the captain of the football team and an eighth grader," Burt reflected. "And you could imagine how the town took to that one!"

"Oh, wow!" Tuck couldn't believe it.

"Yeah, her ma took alot of flack for it. People asking her how she was raising her kid, shit like that," Burt nodded to see if he was getting Tuck's approval.

"Wow, that's all I can say. Bad times, huh?" Tuck sided with the customer.

"Yeah, but that was then this is now. She has someone though." Tuck thought he almost seen a tear from Burt.

"Who is it? Anyone I know?"

"Well, if I had my choice I rather see you with her, but it's your buddy, Irvin Baker." Burt raised his eyebrows along with one side of his mouth. "I don't know why."

"And the last one is for me," Becky proclaimed. "Although, I do have a little left for later." She gave a pleasing smile to Pete, noticed Donna out of the corner of her eye, and quickly looked to Irvin.

"I'll be around until five," Irvin accepted the invitation.

"What's at five?" Becky asked, while holding the straw above the white river.

"I got cows to milk!" Irvin put his arms out, "we could all go milk my cows!"

17

Becky leaned forward and inhaled the powder into her nose, it was her way of ignoring the suggestion. "Oh, good coke." Her eyes moistened from the rush and she sucked in hard, shaking her head.

"Real good stuff," Pat started feeling the numb, not only on her tongue, from the little bit she had tasted, but also through her veins. "Shall we go see where the other two went?"

"Yeah, I can show ya my big dog!" Pete had went to the Humane Society and bought a dog for Donna on Thursday, a one year old Black Lab, and kept him in a cage behind the garage. "Did he bark when you all came up?"

"I didn't hear nothin'," Becky looked at Pat. "Did you?"

"No. You don't have no dog." Pat did not believe him, maybe it was the face he put on.

"Yes, we do, Pat!" Donna jumped out of her chair. "Come on, let's go see Sammy!"

The five of them stood up and filed out, Donna taking the lead, Pete behind her, with Becky and Irvin bringing up the rear. "Irvin, you want to go for a cruise?" Becky had no idea about his on and off relationship with Pat.

"Where to?" Relationships Irvin totally sucked at.

"Come on, Sam's right behind the garage," Pete was out the door, down the steps, and running as if he was a five year old showing off his new dog. Well, in a sense, he was.

Donna ran out after Pete, while Pat hung back checking on Irvin, "You guys coming?"

"Yeah, we're coming," Irvin answered while eyeing Becky.

"Are we staying or going?" Becky pushed, she didn't come all this way for some chit-chat and Irvin stood as her likely candidate for getting a little. "I'll make it worth your while."

Irvin pushed his envelope, "should I stay or should I go, Pat will always be here," he thought to himself as if he donned a crown.

Pat stood in the middle of the driveway for a second and gave up on waiting for the other two to come out, but as soon as she turned around—'RUFF!' Dog paws on her chest. "Oh my, God!" Pete and Donna came running from behind the garage. "Is this Sammy?" Pat fluffed his ears as he tried nuzzling and licking her face. "Good Dog."

Becky and Irvin came out of the cabin, "Sammy, what a cute dog," Becky couldn't resist.

Sammy was down from Pat, up the steps to Becky, back down the steps, stopped not knowing who to go, so he just took off running. Around the garage, around the cabin, around the garage, a quick side-step towards Pat and Donna, around the cabin once more, "and here he comes!" Pete yelled, hands held high, and like a bolt of lightning he took off down the path. "There's my dawg!"

"Our dog, Pete!" Donna corrected, but she knew all about man's best friend.

"Well, we were going down there anyway," Pat remarked.

"Yep, let's go!" Pete took off running.

"Here, Becky, did you say we could have some of those coolers?" Pat asked.

"Yeah, I'll get 'em for ya," she trotted over to the car, popped the trunk, and told Pat to take the whole cooler. Berry, Lime, and Kiwi sitting on ice. "I think we're going for a cruise," she pointed her eyes to Irvin.

"Oh," Pat swallowed," if that's what you want to do." She said while looking at Becky, but Irvin knew it was meant for him.

"So, Irvin, are you ready?" Becky repeated, this time in voice. "Maybe we'll go to that spot Simon showed me last time I was here." Spoken like a true Southern Belle, including body language.

"Donna, want to help me with this cooler," Pat couldn't bare to watch her so-called friend make a fool of herself, but, then again, how long had she been waiting for this farmboy. "As soon as we get to the lake I'll twist up another fatty, for some reason I just lost my buzz." Pat grabbed one handle and Donna the other as they ventured towards the lake. "Donna, do you still have that cat?"

"Oh, yeah, Burnie's around here somewhere," Donna combed the air with her left arm. "Did I ever tell you how he got his name?" The two ladies kept walking, chatting about a cat and carrying a cooler, destination just a few yards ahead. A beautiful day, bright sunlight, good people, nothing better than having a lake right down a private path, Pete and donna called it 'Paradise'.

"Say, just hold on, Irvin," Becky jumped back out of Irvin's truck, seeing the two figures disappear down the path, "I gotta get my purse."

18

"Okay, I can wait." Irvin had something up his sleeve, maybe it was the drugs and the alcohol making him play such foolish games. Did Becky really know what she was in for? Maybe she didn't much care, either.

Becky went back into the cabin, grabbed her purse, and noticed Pete's tray under the couch. She knew it had been there, but in her mind it seemed like more of a game if she could tell Irvin "it just happened to be there, waiting for me to take". She brought it out from under the couch and dissected it, "just a little—he won't miss it." She took out her cigarette pack and took off the outer wrapper, placing the marijuana into it, she then put the outer wrapper and its contents back into the cigarette pack, "now I'm ready, thanks Pete." She headed out the door and jumped into Irvin's truck, "Okay, I just had to get my purse."

THE LION OR THE LAMB   5/19

Once the cards are dealt out, being it Poker, Black Jack, or Crazy 8, is it still a card game or merely a game of guessing expressions. Who's holding the Joker?

"Here, Tuck, fill me up another," Burt held his mug, "but give me a new mug."

"Sure, thing," Tuck listened to his customers. "Irvin and Pat? Still hard to believe."

"Ah, ya might as well just forget about it. The kid has more money than the two of us put together...and then some," Burt threw in a likely reason for Pat's interest.

"Man, if that's all she's after."

"Well, good money buys good drugs," Burt overstepped.

"You saying Pat would go after the drugs? A woman like that only goes after the hard stuff: cocaine, meth, ecstasy. And you're saying Pat's on it?"

"Well, she's done it," Burt held to his assessment.

Simon and Kim had been strolling along the shoreline, skipping small stones over the thin layer of ice covering the lake, "Wonder if she'll melt today," Simon refereed to the ice and the nice temperature. "They say it's supposed to get close to seventy today and then plummet by early morning, creating a possible snow storm."

"You're kidding!" Kim wasn't one to keep up on the daily news, always sad stories, murders, divorces, and pictures of models she used to work with.

"Nope!" Simon threw a big rock—"Ka-plush!", creating a hole in the ice. "All right!"

"You're silly, Simon," Kim laughed. "Think the others are coming down to the lake?"

"They should be. Them and their coke, I just don't get it. If you want to get up, just get out and smell the fresh air." Simon raised his arms and created a rainbow.

"Amen to that!" Kim agreed, "Let's go back to the path."

Pete had tried keeping up with Sammy to no avail, that dog darted throughout the bushes, looped around a tree, cut to the right, cut to the left, and sprang across the path, almost taking Pete out. Pete bent over in laughter, hand to his forehead, straightened back up, and yelled, "You big ole Dawg!" It was a man and his best friend, a boy with his childhood dream, could it get any better?

Donna and Pat approached the laughing man, "Is he wearing you out?"

"Heck no. I've been waiting for this day," Pete seemed as though a proud father, beaming with confidence, and acknowledging his dreams come true. Sam came running and leaped over the cooler, "All right!"

"Pete," Donna asked with a punch to Pete's shoulder, "you seen Simon and Kim?"

"Nope, not yet."

"Well, you take after Sammy, we're going to the lake," Donna confirmed, grabbing a handle. Pat grabbed the other handle and they strolled to the lake, only forty yards ahead. "I'm getting thirsty."

Heading out of the driveway, Irvin and Becky were about to have an excursion of their own, sort of a bonus added to the day. Kim had been nagging lately, telling Becky she was going out too often and playing too close to the edge. Becky needed space, she almost moved in with a guy she had just met a couple of months earlier. At this point of time Becky could be moving on at any time.

"Glad we're out of there,' Becky opened her window for some fresh air and let her hair blow with the incoming wind.

"Really?" Irvin couldn't believe someone, other than himself, would rather leave a party than to stay, anyway Pete's party.

"It's just Kim. And Donna. And Simon," Becky giving pause behind each name and searching for another.

"No way?" Irvin cut into her searching, "Everyone likes Simon, but me." Irvin tapped his chest.

"Simon's not that bad. It's just that we slept together once, and now it's very uncomfortable to be around him."

"You slept with Simon?" Irvin's eyes widened in complete surprise.

"Well, we actually went skinny-dipping and tried to have sex," Becky came back to the truth.

"What do you mean? You tried to have sex," Irvin did not understand.

20

"We tried, but because of the water and as drunk as Simon was, nevertheless the dope we all smoked," Becky laughed lightly, not sure if it was out of embarrassment or humility, "Simon couldn't get it up!" she blushed, put her hand to her mouth and turned towards the window. "I don't believe I just said that."

"Oh, man," Irvin squeezed the steering wheel, "do I have one on him!"

"Now, wait a minute. Why would you say that?" Becky could not take back what she had said.

"Hey, the guy deserves it!"

"What has he ever done to you?" Becky wanted evidence for revenge.

"He's just Simon, just the name gets me," Irvin wrinkled his face in disgust.

"Here, turn in right here!" Becky directed, vocally and with her outstretched arm in front of Irvin's face. "This is where me and Simon went."

Irvin slammed on the brakes, "Man, want me to have an accident?"

"Just turn in here. There's a small clearing next to the lake. I brought some extra smoke and I have some of that powder left," Becky smiled, she was hoping all talk of Simon had came to an end. She was here to have fun, let go, and possibly get laid.

"You sure no one will see us?" Irvin still a little nervous. Becky had just took the upper bid with her startling arm maneuver and forwardness. Would the four aces Becky held beat out the joker in Irvin's hand? At this stage of the game, he knew he had lost the lead.

"Go up a little further, then. By the way it looks," she noticed tire tracks, "someone else has been coming back here." She looked at Irvin instating it may be his tracks.

"No," he shook his head, "I haven't been back here. Well, I used to a long time ago."

"And why not, lately? Are you scared to be seen?" Becky moved to the middle of the bench seat, "you can pull over anytime you want." She reached over and unbuttoned his shirt, from the top down.

"Okay," he started to sweat after the second button and grabbed her hand, "just let me pull in here." He drove into a small clearing and turned the keys. "No one will see us back here."

"Shall we continue?" her smile, her eyes, her wanting.

"Uh, sure," his voice cracking, his nerves, his thoughts of Pat. He lifted his arm around Becky and leaned back, trying to relax. She undid the buttons, yanked his shirt out of his jeans to get the last one, and parted his shirt exposing his chest. She rubbed his nipples gently, then bent down to lick them, very gently. She blew softly over his whole chest and then started to blow her way down. With one hand she undid his jeans, button first and then the zipper. "Oohh, Magic," as she stroked his hidden muscle. She put her hand inside of his underwear and cupped his solid marbles, "Oohh, Magic," she whispered in his ear and then bit down softly. "I want you," her hand back around his muscle, squeezing, "take me, farmboy!"

Irvin's nerves were jumping, but his heart nearly stopped, "Uh, you're good." His one hand brushed through her hair, while the other one couldn't let go of making a fist.

"Take me, Magic!" She straddled her leg and now sat on Irvin's lap, rubbing his taught muscle between her legs, up and down. She had a wild glare, scratched her fingernails down his chest, and leaned forward with a powerful French kiss.

Irvin was out of orbit, his mind dizzy, all but one of his muscles trembling, the other just stood ready to explode, "I can't!"

Becky sat up, the moment lost, "And you call yourself a man, hmph. I should have known you're nothing more than a cowboy." She got off his lap, grabbed her purse, and let herself out of the truck.

"Hey, I'm sorry, but I couldn't do it," Irvin tried his hand at explaining. "You see me and Pat...."

"What? You and Pat, and you led me on?" Becky was pissed.

"I know," Irvin done up his jeans and opened his door, "I'm a fool for trying."

"Huh, you don't know the just of it," Becky shook her head, looked towards the lake, and back at Irvin, "Pat could have killed me right there on the spot, asshole!"

"I thought you knew," Irvin thought playing stupid would get him out of this mess. "Didn't she tell you?" He climbed out of the truck, hands up in surrender mode.

"No, she didn't," hands on hips. "Last thing I heard of you was that you slept with Kim!"

Irvin bent his head to the ground, "Another mistake."

21

"And Pat puts up with this shit? You are one lucky jerk."

"Hey, I said I'm sorry."

"Tell that to her. That's if she'll still talk to ya!"

Irvin held out his hand, "Truce? I mean between us two. At least I stopped before we got to far."

"What is too far?" Becky slapped his hand. "You best clear up your boundaries with your girlfriend. I just hope she has no intention of kicking my ass." She walked down to the lake's edge, shaking her head, and then she spun around, "How many times have you slept around on her?"

"Just that once, with Kim."

"And how many times do you play with other women in front of her?"

"I don't know."

"You are sick!" Becky meant it. "Do you think you're God, that you can just go around pinching girls in the ass and coming on to them, while your best girl just stands there?"

"Well," Irvin was getting his just dessert, "I've only done it a few times."

"And you think it's all right?"

"No one ever told me different," he spoke the truth, an only child with all the luxuries of being spoiled, everything given to him, except what mattered most—discipline and love.

Becky stared into his eyes, she could tell he had been alone, "I know what you mean." She calmed down, "Being spoiled is not what it's made out to be. You wanna grab my purse for me?" Irvin obliged and grabbed her purse, then strolled down to the edge of the lake by her. "Thanks, Magic," a shallow tear crawled down her cheek, "Life can really suck sometimes."

"It's okay," he put his hand around her, "we can always be friends."

Simon and Kim reached the path at the same time Pat and Donna arrived, "All right, ladies, I need another cooler!"

"So, Kim, Simon been telling you any stories?" Pat, the investigator, reporter.

"No, he hasn't been saying nothing." Kim could keep secrets.

"Nothing at all?" Donna provoked, backing up Pat. She needed someone on her side, besides Pete.

"Ladies!" Simon exclaimed, "What do you want to hear? I can tell you a story about most anything." Simon, the struggling playwright, musician, game designer, and production worker.

"Oh, shush, you loony," Donna might have lost trust in him, after the Becky thing, but she still liked his comedy and friendship. She grabbed a cold-one out of the cooler and handed another to Pat.

"I'm serious. I can dance, sing, tell riddles," he played Gene Kelley once in a class play and figures his resume' is filled. "Where's Pete, Becky, and Irvin?"

"Well, Pete should be coming right along," Donna pointed down the path, "and Becky took Irvin for a little cruise."

"It was more Irvin took her," Pat did not hide the fact Irvin couldn't back down from an invitation.

"Oh," Simon knew about Pat and Irvin, but kept it to himself. "But you have the smoke, right?"

Pat smiled with attention, "Yes I do." She had stuffed the bag into her pocket, leaving her purse at the cabin. "Oh, shit. I forgot to bring papers."

"No problem, I'll be right back," Simon volunteered his foot speed. "They're in your purse, right? The black one?"

"Yes! Thank you, Simon!" Maybe he wasn't such a bad guy, after all. Maybe it was time Pat started listening to herself, rather than to those around her, especially Irvin.

Simon went running down the path and almost got side-swiped by a black flash, Sammy, "Holy cats!. Where'd you come from?"

Pete seen the action and left out a roar, "Way to go, Sammy!"

"That your dog?" Simon came to a stop. "Cool!"

"Yeah," Pete walked up to Simon. "Got him a few days ago. Donna wanted a one, so, I got her one." Simple logic is all Pete needed.

Simon approved, "You're a good man. Well, I gotta go get Pat's purse. I'll be right back."

"Watch out for the dog!"

"So, you think Serby'll come marching in here, today?" Tuck asked Burt, knowing he was Serby's best friend and confidant.

22

"No, he's off to some wedding in the cities. Why?"

"Just asking, no real reason." Tuck's mind was stuck with boredom. "How can you sit in here all day, especially with the sun shining?"

Burt just shrugged his shoulders, "Maybe I've seen enough sunshine."

"Never!" Tuck wiped down the bar thinking to himself, "why did that couple leave, at least they were playing some good tunes", he then threw the remote control in Burt's direction, "what should we snack on next?"

"Now, Becky, you're not telling Pat what happened, right?" Irvin could play the game, he just didn't want no one else knowing about it.

"Yeah, right, should I tell her we did it, instead? But that's probably what you want, isn't it?"

"No," poor confused Irvin, "I just want...."

"What, Irvin?" Becky did not come home to baby-sit. "How about we just tell her the truth? How about you telling her the truth?" she wanted no part of 'domestic abuse'.

"Okay, I'll tell her the truth. If she believes it."

"Well, if you wouldn't have brought me out here in the first place, Gomer." She knocked him along the side of his head. "But since we're here," she opened her purse, "glass or plastic?"

Simon darted into the cabin, grabbed the purse, and ran back out towards the lake. Pete finally made it up to the ladies and asked for a wine cooler. Sammy, he was still running around in the soft breeze and sunshine. Kim and Pat had taken a seat on a huge rock, "So, do you miss Mayville?"

"Sort of," Kim could not deny. "I mean, that's why I came back. To see how things were."

"And you might stay?" Pat's mouth lifted in the corners.

"Don't push to any conclusions," Kim held her hands out. "I'm only in the thinking stage."

"And what have you been thinking about?" Pat pressed on. Donna came over and took a rock next to them, while Pete toyed around with the ice. Sammy was taking a break, finding some shade by an old Oak tree.

"I don't know. It's just been a hell of a month."

"And you're hiding something from me, aren't you?" Pat could tell.

"Sort of, but sort of not," Kim tried keeping in, keeping her problems to herself.

"Have you heard from Marty?" Marty had been Kim's agent in the early years, setting her up with photo-shoots, magazines, etc., but then he took his status a little too far. He became a control-freak, as Kim once put it, watching her weight and expanding on her schedule, while trying to be her lover and bookkeeper. She did end up firing him and going through the court system on harassment charges, minor assault, and child custody. They shared one boy, Michael Scott, who, last Kim knew, about three years ago, lived with Marty's parents.

"No, I haven't heard him," Pat had struck a nerve. "But I have been thinking about Mikey."

"I'm sorry," Pat apologized. "I didn't mean to bring up the bad."

"I know, Pat, you've always been my best friend." Kim put her arm around Pat and squeezed.

Simon came running down the path and into the clearing, "Here's your purse."

"You brought the whole thing?"

"Hey, I'm not digging into no purse."

"Okay, well, thanks, Simon," Pat laughed, guys were always afraid to get something out of her purse, as if some curse came along with the task. She opened her purse and dug out the baggie, "Time to smoke one!"

Simon jogged over to Pete, about twenty feet down the shoreline, "What you doing?"

"Just trying to break up the ice."

"Hear it's supposed to snow tonight." Simon picked up a stick and joined in with Pete.

"Get out , there ain't gonna be no snow. Look at the sky," Pete pointed his stick upwards.

"Things'll change," Simon kept breaking up the ice, never looking up.

Since Irvin couldn't make up his mind, Becky matched—putting a little cocaine with the marijuana.

She found an extra paper at the bottom of her purse, and after sprinkling it, twisted it up. "Here, you can light on, since you did stop yourself from getting us both killed!" She still couldn't believe it happened.

23

"So, all's forgotten," he held up the joint, grinning with relief. He reached in his pocket and brought out a lighter, torched the 'drug stick', inhaled, and handed it to Becky, "Where the green grass grows...."

"Hey, guys, come and get it!" Pat yelled toward the ice-breakers. "The fat-cabin is waiting!"

Pete dropped his stick and came running, Simon kept his stick and put his gear into 'stroll', Sammy had fallen asleep, but now had his ears up and his tail wagging. The girls were sitting on their respective rocks, Pat looking for a lighter. "I got that!" Pete pulled a lighter from his pocket and tossed it to Pat. "Good catch!"

Donna relaxed with a sunbeam, warm, along with a gentle breeze. The setting couldn't get more inviting, the perfect day. Kim reached for the lighted joint after Pat took a hit, "Maybe, I've been needing this." She drew on the cabin deeply, shut her eyes, and tried to drift. "Here you go..." as she passed it on Pete, she then took a drink from her wine cooler, "Did I tell you I might be staying?" she gazed at Pat.

Pat laughed, but kept the answer to herself. Simon approached Pete, but declined on the joint, so Pete handed it to Donna. She didn't hesitate and enjoyed the taste, "I'm glad we have company today. Aren't you Peter?" her mood was getting mischievous, in a teasing way.

Pete smiled and then noticed, "Weren't there two of you?"

Kim looked up as she felt someone staring at her, "What?"

"Weren't you with another girl?" Pete repeated, and now everyone questioned Pete with their expressions, not remembering Pete had been with Sammy when Becky and Irvin took off.

"Oh, Becky!" Pat was the first to re-think the situation. "She left with your buddy about an hour ago. They're probably milking cows." She rather make light of the situation then to call Irvin a bad name and regret it later, for she did trust him. It was Becky she knew as the firecracker.

"Here, farmboy, torch it!" Becky handed the 'twinkie' to Irvin. "I rolled it, you light it. You do have a lighter, don't you?" She noticed him digging around his pockets.

"Well, I did have one. I must have left it at Pete's." He continued searching, but he only had so many pockets, and checking them three times was not going to make any kind of magic. "I don't know."

"Then I'll let you use mine. Here," She gave him the lighter, in such a manner that he would have to touch her, along with a sparkle in her eye. Maybe it was the sun erasing recent memories, but Becky would give it one more shot to land Irvin right where she wanted him, inside—deep inside.

Pete walked over to Donna, handing her the joint and then sitting down beside her, "Here, Honey."

"You two," Pat could not resist, "are so good together. I mean, you really have each other." Pete looked over to Donna, combing her with his eyes and gently resting his hand upon her shoulder.

"Yep, me and my baby," He smiled confidently. Sammy nudged between the two, "and the dog."

Laughter whispered in this small circle, love shown right before them. If we all could be so lucky, sharing dreams, sharing tenderness, sharing fun and laughter, sharing each other, most people would call this beauty, and at Cyprus Lake the experience is amazing. Simon paused his short laughter, stepped back from the circle to get a better focus, and his own memories started taking him places: Becky, Donna, Kansas...

Kim didn't mean to intrude, but Pete's facial features struck her as someone she once met, "Where are you from?" She questioned in his direction. "I don't mean to be nosy but you look familiar, just the way you looked towards her. It's like I met you before." She tried explaining herself without making Donna suspicious, but Pete's resemblance just struck her.

"Now there's a question," he nodded his head, not quite ready to tell a story. "Let's see, born and raised on the north side of Minneapolis.."

"Okay, maybe I've seen you there?" Kim interrupted.

"Well, I haven't been there for at least seven years. I made it to graduation and hit the road!" spoken as if his goal had been accomplished with an extra bonus.

"Where did you go? I mean it's as if I seen you somewhere?" She was bothered with the familiar face, but also the way he had laughed. Donna and Pat egged him on, "Yeah, Pete, where did you go?"

"From high school I journeyed across the border."

24

"You mean Canada?" Pat spoke, surprised, being she thought of going there herself.

"Nope, just Wisconsin."

"Uhh, that's not across the border." Donna punched him in the shoulder, laughing. "You're silly."

"Well, I had to cross somethin' to get there," he tried proving his point. "But then I went down to Gary, Indiana and caught a train."

"You jumped on a train?" Kim couldn't believe the courage it would take to do such a thing.

"Yep. I jumped on a train goin' west. Thought I would end up in Seattle, but....instead, I ended up in Beverly Hills, California."

"Get out!" Pat exclaimed with amazement, she often thought about Hollywood, too. Her, Kim, and Becky all had their dreams, each singing in front of the mirror, modeling in front of each other, swapping clothes and make-up, and school plays—that was their moment.

"Yep! I got me a genuine Hollywood star!" Donna piped in, smiling very proudly, and then giving Pete a one-armed hug. And she was proud of her man, albeit his features were enough to melt any girl, it was also his humor and listening ability, his caring side, that Donna truly adored.

"And from there," Pete cringed under Donna's hug, continuing his personal saga, "I hopped in a car coming back to good old Minnesota. Well, I went broke first. And the car made it to the northern outskirts of Iowa, so, I left the guys I was with and started walking....." he let his conclusion hang.

"Where'd you walk to? You can't just quit," he had all of Pat's interest.

"I walked right up to that spot over there," he pointed across the lake. "Pinched a tent in the afternoon and the next day some farmer came waking me up. Scared the shit out of me. Knocking on my tent with a stick or something. I mean, I thought I was dead!"

"What happened?" Kim no longer thought of his past resemblance, it must have been someone else, but the story being told—wow!

"I finally get up enough nerve and get out of the tent and this guy is just standing there. He asks me where I came from and what my intentions were. I said I had no intentions and wanted to be left alone."

"Then what?" came the chorus.

"He offered me a job. He said I had been wasting my youth and growing old too fast. He would give me a free room and I could help myself to the kitchen. That cabin we're in," he motioned with his finger to Donna and himself, "well, that's the room he gave me."

"And the kitchen," Donna made sure he didn't leave out any pieces, she had heard the story before.

"Yep, and the kitchen. He gave me a ride over here and I haven't seen him since."

"Wow, now that's an amazing story. I need another wine-cooler." Kim walked over to the cooler and pulled out a bottle. "Anyone else need one? There's five left. By the way, where did Simon go?"

"Hey, bartender, give me one more," Burt pushed. His Saturdays usually consisted of a few cold-ones and then back to his shop to catch up on the work he hadn't got done during the week, an oil-change here a brake-job there, but today he just didn't feel the need.

"You've been saying one more for the last hour," Tuck confirmed, but just for conversation purposes.

"Then set up at least three."

"I'm just joking. They'll get warm if I set them all out." Tuck poured a mug full and pushed it down the bar to Burt's waiting hand. "Where is everyone?"

"Oh, they'll come. When you least expect it, they'll come." He took a sip of his beer and sat quietly, or was he just being patient.

Tuck searched around the room for an outlet, something to pick up his spirits, he had shared peanuts, shared the remote control, shared some conversation, but all with one customer. He needed someone to walk through that door.

"You hear 'em coming?" Burt asked softly, over the top of his mug. Tuck heard him, but didn't know if he really wanted to—was Burt going psycho?

How many moments are in a day? Is there two parts to a day or sometimes more? You have morning, afternoon, and evening. Do they come with a difference?

Some days are over in a flash, yet some seem to last forever. Is it the season, the song, or the harmony amongst ourselves?

On a good sun-filled day you can trust everyone. Please, remember to walk gently into the night.

Simon walked gently amongst the trees, there was still small patches of snow found in the shaded areas. It was a bit cooler than in the wide-open, but he felt drawn to its inner beauty, he was a searcher, and felt compelled to know the world's answers. Where did we come from, where are we all going, and what are we doing in the meantime. Is there certain tests to pass? And how many tests are there? He kept thinking to himself as he walked, looking up and looking down. He stopped to watch a squirrel run, stop, run, and made a clicking noise to get its attention. He observed the birds and listened to their song. He stopped and bent his head down, a white feather—a spiritual sign lay at his feet, he picked it up and gently combed it, his day had been accomplished, his lesson for the day had been absorbed—appreciate the beauty around oneself. He smiled as he turned his head toward the sky, "Thank you....." He then affixed the feather to his pocket, as if putting a medal upon his chest.

"How'd you like the taste of that, Magic?" as if nicknames would help Becky get her wish.

"My mouth is totally numb."

"Yeah, but how do you like the taste," she brushed her hair back with her hand and gave an expression of rejection.

"It tasted all right." It actually had a chalk taste, but Irvin didn't want to hurt no feelings. "I mean it was good. But if I had something to drink it would be even better." He had tired of her ploys and would rather be back with the rest of them over at Pete's.

"I can give you something else to taste," she leaned sideways, towards boy-wonder, licking her lips.

"Becky, I thought we went down that road," in a subtle whine, as if a small gopher caught in a trap.

"And you did say no one would know anything. Besides, Magic," her eyes twinkled, "how long have we been away? Don't you think Pat is already suspicious?"

Irvin stood up, "You're right, maybe we should just go back!"

"And I thought you were a man." Becky now stood up and brushed off her butt, "The grass was still wet, is my butt wet?" she turned around, back facing him.

"Just a little, nothin' I can do." He walked back to the truck, "Come on, I need something to drink." Becky inhaled and blew out, then joined Irvin in the truck. "Do you have everything?"

"Yes, Mr. Irvin, I have everything," she opened her window all the way down, she had wasted enough of her energy on this farm-boy.

It seemed Kim was the only one concerned about Simon's whereabouts, the others had experienced his disappearing act before. So, she wandered into the trees. The others enjoyed the rays coming down, Pete and Donna had Sam running back and forth trying to decide which stick to go after, and Pat took it easy, stretching out on the big rock—wiping all her worries away, as few as she had. Her eyes were closed, but she was wide awake. She drifted back to high school, the guys in her life, her friends and co-workers, her mom, and she smiled, totally relaxed. She took her hands from her stomach and let them hang. Her right hand landing on something furry, and it moved!

Pat sat up quickly and looked down where her hand had been, "Oh, my! Is this your cat?"

"Simon, I see you!" Kim called out, making out a silhoute in the distance.

"Well, I see you, too!" he yelled back and started running towards her. He darted around small twigs and hurdled a tree stump, trying to show-off his athletic ability.

Kim laughed at his boyish nature, but was impressed with his balance and speed. She had volunteered, years earlier, at the YMCA in Minneapolis with gymnastics. That was before her modeling career took off, when she could afford spending time with children. "You're gonna fall!"

26

As soon as she said it, Simon misplaced his left foot and went into a tumble, head under feet and feet back on the ground. He stretched his arms out above him as if coming off the pummel horse in pure '10' form. "How was that?"

"Amazing!" Kim clapped her hands. "I have never seen anyone do such a stunt."

"Accidents happen." He walked over to Kim and gave her a hug, it just seemed right. He held her close, but not tight, saying nothing. She hugged him back, not quite sure of the circumstance, but she knew there was nothing to lose. After a brief moment of silence he let go, "are the others still out here?"

At least the jukebox was being played, again. The bad part of it being played was that it was a wedding party playing it. A group of at least twenty wanting shots, latest fads, and Kitty cocktails, nice and sticky. "Burt, why aren't you a bartender?" Tuck asked between a Kitty cocktail and wiping his hands of the grenadine and cherry juice.

"I know you know the answer to that." Burt acknowledged and gave the right answer.

The life of a bartender, one minute your down and the next minute your up, a regular roller coaster, except you're getting paid to ride on this one. And the fringe benefits: low cut dresses leaning over your bar, teasing expressions, personal questions, and an occasional napkin left behind with a phone number. "Yeah, I could be talking to myself," Tuck realized to himself after getting an order for a Brandy Manhattan and a Screwdriver from a slender blonde with crystal blue eyes. He also learned that an order for two drinks mostly meant she was not alone. His number one rule— 'Don't get involved'.

Irvin and Becky turned into the driveway, no words had been spoken since leaving their hiding place. "So, nothing happened, right?" Becky felt a little fear, or mistrust, concerning Irvin. He might say they did something just to get Pat jealous.

"No!" He parked the truck in front of the cabin. "Maybe, I should just go home. I don't need to be taking any chances in front of Pat, with you!" he exclaimed directly to Becky's face.

"By time someone has taught you a lesson," she got out of the truck and slammed the door. "Go home to your cows! I don't know if it's such a good idea I let you go out with my friend, anyway!"

Irvin got out of the truck and ran around the front end, grabbing Becky's arm, "Hey, I'm the one who put a stop to us!"

"Yeah, well, you're also the one who provoked the whole thing. So, put that in your pipe and smoke it!" she tore herself loose from his grasp and began walking towards the lake. After walking about fifteen feet she turned around, Irvin still stood in the same place, "Well, are you coming?"

Kim and Simon came upon Pete first, "Hey, you find nature-boy!" Pete had taken residents on a small rock, sucking down a wine cooler while playing with Sam's ears. Donna had Burnie, her black and white tomcat, in her arms, and Pat gazed out over the ice-covered lake. Until she noticed Simon.

"Simon, where have you been?" she only sounded like a mother, but she was actually just shitting with the guy. She stood up from her rock, "Did you see any strange creatures?" Her and Simon had made a deal, I can give you shit and you can give me shit, nothing serious, and nothing harmed.

"Yeah, this one-horned purple thing." Simon stretched his arms upward and stood on his tip-toes.

Kim stepped away from him, "You didn't tell me."

Pat laughed, rather choked, being she had just taken a drink. "Don't do that when I just took a drink. Oh, man." She swore she had wine-cooler coming out of her nose. They all laughed, even the cat wore a grin.

"What's so funny?" came the question from Irvin as he approached the clearing.

Pat stopped and stared directly into his eyes, "What's it matter?"

Irvin swallowed and started to turn away, but Becky grabbed onto him. "You're not leaving that fast, I think you owe someone an apology," she demanded. Pat was struck with Becky's reaction, "Did she actually say no?"

"Well?" Becky questioned the key witness, "Are you going to talk to her?"

"Um, Pat, can I, I mean....can we?"

"What is it Mr. Baker, cat got your tongue?" Pat was ready to make him sweat, and to sweat in front of everyone. Donna giggled as she squeezed the cat. Pete kept his mind focused on the dog, but

27

noticing he was in ear-shot distance, grabbed the dog by his collar and walked away from the heat. Simon motioned to Kim and they both sat on a rock facing the truth.

"No, there's no cat." Irvin tried to be funny.

"Oh, but there is a cat!" Donna held up her fifteen pound feline.

"So, Becky," Pat continued the interrogation, "did you have fun with the cows?"

"We didn't see any cows."

"Oh, so you never made it that far?" Ask one question to get an answer for another one, "So, how far did you make it?" and then come back with a direct hit.

"Pat," Irvin recoiled and tried snapping back, "I just want to talk with you," but he didn't have much to recoil with.

"I tell you what, farm-boy," she walked over to him and put her index finger in the middle of his chest, "there is no next time to talk about. If you want to play games in front of my friends, well, I don't want you. I want a man not a boy!" She turned away and then looked back and squared up her shoulders, "Maybe it would be best if you just leave." He stood and listened, then turned. "Don't even think about me giving you another chance. I've had it!"

He started walking, head forward, but eyes to the ground, "I messed up," he mumbled to himself, "If it wasn't for Becky, I wouldn't be in this spot." He kicked the ground as he walked.

"You all right, Pat?" Donna asked. In this one afternoon, although there had been others, Pat grew on her. She really liked what she saw, a caring, understanding, and yet, carefree person. Now Donna would find out how strong Pat was.

"I'll be fine," Kim had gotten up from her rock and held out her arms. Pat fell into them, "such an asshole. When am I gonna grow up?"

"It's okay," Kim whispered as soft as the brush strokes she was administering to Pat's back. Becky came over and rubbed Pat's shoulder.

"I'm sorry, I'm truly sorry." Pat backed away from Kim and stared at Becky. "I'm sorry, Patty, but nothing happened. I swear, he wouldn't do it."

"And who are you? Taking him for a ride and trying to get a little," Pat put all the blame on Becky. Irvin had left, and besides, didn't Becky say Irvin wouldn't do anything. Then who was pushing him, "Aren't you supposed to be my friend?"

"And I am. I just got carried away, he's a nice guy," Becky went too far.

"Oh, so you did try to get him?"

"Pat, I had no idea you two were together!" she yelled it before Pat could get close enough to slap her. "I mean, do you always hide secrets? Why didn't you tell me about him?"

"Because of the last time you two were here!" Now she got Kim involved.

"Have you ever tried to put the blame on Irvin?" Kim felt the dagger go into her back after Pat's last statement, and it didn't feel good. "He was all over me that night!"

Pat bowed her head and raised her hand to her forehead, "I know. He told me."

"And you went back to him?" Kim was caught in disbelief.

"I couldn't help it." Tears were now coming down Pat's face, an understanding woman with a big heart. "He needed someone and I was here. Don't you get it?"

"Pat, you are not his mother." Becky tried to ease the pain.

"Then who is? His real mom is dead." Pat had been holding it in for some time, ever since Irvin's parents were killed in an auto accident five years ago. "That's all I wanted, just to be his friend, but then he lost his family and I was all he had. He's mixed up, but how can I blame him?"

"So, you just blame yourself and he gets by with murder?" Kim had her list of mistakes and on that list, right at the top, was abuse—verbal, written, and physical. "Don't you know what's he holding back?" Pat wiped away the tears and lifted her eyes to meet Kim's. "Patty, we've missed you."

Irvin never looked back as he approached his truck. He opened the door, jumped in, and turned the key. "I need some good music," he reached into the glove box to find some heavy-metal, it went with his mood. Upon finding his special disc, he slipped it into the CD player and cranked up the volume. He put the transmission in 'Drive' and took a glance out the side window, "What?" Simon stared back. Irvin rolled down his window, "You freak! What do you want?"

"It's not me that wants anything, but you," Simon carried a very serious expression. "What exactly are you running from?"

28

"You are nuts! Why don't you just leave me alone!" Irvin pushed down on the accelerator and made a rough U-turn in the middle of the yard. He glared back at Simon on his way out, "Leave me alone!"

Simon tilted his head toward the sky, the clouds began moving in, "Please, be with him, for he is only a frightened child."

Irvin got to the end of the driveway, a quick stop, and then pushed the accelerator to the floor sending stones twenty feet behind him. Inside the cab he had the volume as high as it could get (insert Heavy Metal—loud), but inside his mind lay confusion, fear, and jealousy.

Donna had reached into the cooler and pulled out the last beverage. She didn't open it, but rather stood holding it for Pat's sake, who was involved in a group hug with Kim and Becky. Sometimes we need to be touched, sometimes we need to be held. Pete still remained at a distance, the whole sister-love thing was not his area, besides, Sammy and Burnie were doing some crazy tactics, it was hilarious!

Pat backed up from the huddle, wiping away the last of her tears, "Okay, enough crying!" And there was Donna, ready with the beverage. "I think I still have some, but thanks anyway." She gave Donna a smile and walked over to the rock carrying her bottle, "Yep, still a little in here!" Her face sparkled as if glitter had been put there, the sun's rays and tears created a nice shine or was it the smile her eyes were holding. "A toast to my friends," she held up her bottle, "Thank you!" They all grabbed their bottles, Donna handing the last one over to Becky, raised them in unison, and clicked them together. They all tipped their bottles, a taste of Berry along with a taste of triumph. Bringing their bottles back together, and saying as a chorus, "To a Special Day!" in which they broke into laughter.

Kim stumbled back to her rock and sat down, giggling. Pat and Becky held a truce, "All is forgiven and forgotten," Pat promised and Becky agreed. Donna went running down the shoreline towards Pete. The afternoon was coming to a close. The clouds were rolling in as the clock struck

4:45 p.m. and a chill hung in the air. Simon reappeared from the path. "Where have you been?"

"Around."

"Oh," Pat knew not to ask details, not with Simon. She looked over the lake and shivered.

"Yeah, it's gonna get cold soon," Simon agreed with Pat's shivers. He had no weather degree, but usually came close with his predictions. "They've even been talking about snow."

"No way!" Kim exclaimed. "What channel were you watching?"

Simon shrugged his shoulders, remaining silent, and then walked over to the cooler, opening it, "All's gone, huh?"

"I guess so, Smarty!" Becky answered, watching every move Simon had been making. "You said you couldn't drink, anyway."

Simon shrugged his shoulders, again, "You got me there. Thanks for not letting me fall."

"Hey, Simon, guess you were right!" Pete hollered as he and Donna came walking back up the shore. "Guess it's gonna rain, or something."

Simon nodded his head then looked toward the sky, "Yup. She's gonna do something."

"I guess we better make plans," Pat suggested, "I don't want to be caught out here in the rain. Besides, the coolers are all gone."

"There's always Serby's!" Simon didn't drink, but he found nothing wrong with a little advertisement, especially when he thought of Tuck and how bored he might be in an empty bar.

"Let's go!" Kim jumped to her feet. Becky followed by standing up and walking towards the path.

Pat motioned to Donna about the cooler.

"Nope, someone else is going to have to help you with that, we're staying out here a little longer," Donna didn't mind the rain, especially with Pete and her animals next to her. "You never know, maybe we'll get a light show!" Her expression for a lightning storm.

Kim stepped forward and took a handle, "All you have to do is ask."

"Well, we'll see you guys!" Simon waved and headed down the path. The three ladies did likewise. Up the path they went, in a slow tempo, taking in the details of the thick tree-line. The shadows melted together, the sun disappearing into the clouds, the coolness came back, and the wind began to pick up. "There could be a snowstorm, tonight."

29

"Don't be using such language, Mr. Simon!" Kim had no intentions of going back to Minneapolis tonight, but she wouldn't mind going back tomorrow, and knowing how the snow fell in this part of the prairie they could be here another week. Simon softly laughed and continued taking in the scenery.

"Just me and my hunk!" Donna grabbed Pete's arm and then whispered into his ear, "you want to make out?" His eyes spoke with agreement. They turned towards each other and tightly embraced, their lips met and their tongues started to explore, the light-show had begun (close your eyes to fantasy).

Irvin turned up his driveway with a fish-tail, "Women! Man, I gotta have a drink." His temper soared and his actions were becoming violent. "And who does that Simon think he is?" His mind wondered between love and hate. Did Pat mean what she said, even though she has said it before? Was Simon moving in on her or was he just being nosy? "Man, I'm just staying away from those people!" He parked the truck next to the barn and jumped out, slamming the door behind him, kicking the ground, and then running into the barn. He had a bottle of his favorite stashed in the milk room, "There we go. Time for a little Captain!"

"Well, Burt, you said they would come," Tuck graded Burt with an A+. Serby's was in full swing with more and more of the wedding party entering through it's door. But when would the departures start? Right when a bartender gets used to the crowd and feels the rhythm, pouring, smiling, dancing, things tend to change—drastically!

"Let's go gang! The wedding party is leaving!" One thing about a wedding party, it doesn't matter if they have finished their drinks, or if they started talking to a stranger, when the train is leaving it's time to go! "Next stop, Hontra!" The place emptied out quicker than butter melting in sunshine.

"Um, what were you saying, Tuck? I didn't hear you?" Burt being serious. Tuck took the rag, which he had been wiping his hands with, thought about it for a second, and then threw it at Burt's face. Burt caught it one-handed and grinned, "Now I'm getting to like ya."

"Shit! Don't be saying things like that. I don't need no one liking me." Tuck cleaned up the empties and not-so empties, getting ready for the next round. "Burt, do you have a home?"

"Yeah, I have a home."

"Just wondering." Tuck pocketed the loose change left on the tables, not bad for a half-hours work. Tips usually told Tuck how his service measured up, sometimes it was just the personality or the ten percent tradition, but Tuck counted it as a grade. "I'll take a B-."

"What you talkin' about?" Burt listened.

"Oh nothing!" Tuck moved on to the next table, "Cool, two bucks!"

"Say, what should I play on the jukebox?" Burt stood up from his stool, leaving a butt imprint.

"Excuse me, you're playing the box?" Tuck had never seen this happen before, nevertheless Burt getting up from his stool.

"What the hay? I've got some loose change." Burt sauntered over to the jukebox and looked it over, "What's your preference, Country or Rock?"

"Play 2422 (insert your favorite Country/Rock song)" Tuck's afternoon had come to an end and he stood ready to kick it in! "You ready to jam!"

Is it your first name or your last name making you noticed? The middle name you want to put first.

Does your mood change when given a nickname, how about changing your name when married? Only one person knows who you are and you have to visit a mirror to talk with them, "Mirror, mirror on the wall, who is the fairest of them all...."

Change your name for a day, maybe for the night, try on someone else's shoes.

"Yeah, the clouds are looking pretty dark," Simon couldn't leave the weather alone, or was he just making sure the others were listening to him. He approached the car along with the three ladies. Becky jumped in and popped the trunk, then started the engine. Kim and Pat lifted the cooler into the trunk .

"Simon, is that all you're concerned about?" Kim asked out of curiousity, she knew there was more than he was letting show. "I mean, wants your interests?"

"Come on, you two," Pat demanded, "you can talk on the way back to town."

Kim nodded to Pat's demands and came around to the passenger side, getting in the backseat. Becky lifted her seat forward to let Simon in. Pat took the navigation seat, although there were no directions to be given, and Becky took the wheel. She turned on the ignition and backed away from the garage. Another memory left behind and another moment straight ahead.

"So, Simon, what's your interests?" Kim picked up where she had left off.

"Sports, books, indian literature, cloud formations, rainbows, animals, and the human mind." He could have went on, but knew when enough was enough.

"Oh, is that all? Well, how about those indians?" Kim picked a category, in spite of her lack of education. She did graduate from high school and modeling school, but realized it was her body and not her mind getting her the paycheck.

"We talking Cleveland?" Sarcastic Simon, playing with the lady.

"Cleveland? What's that have to do with indians? Is that where they came from?" Kim threw out a few suggestions trying not to look stupid.

"No, I thought you were talking baseball."

"Uh, you....I oughtta, but I won't," Kim raised her hand. "I'm not talking baseball!"

"What's going on back there?" Pat joined in turning towards the backseat. "Do we have to let you two walk back?" Becky glanced in the rearview mirror and grinned.

"No! Simon's just being a shithead!" Kim emphasised.

"You wanted to know about the indians, and I thought you meant baseball."

"So, it's a communication thing?" Pat stated, correctly. "You have to watch him, he's sneaky." She then turned back around, her lesson to Kim being given. "What station you want to hear?" she asked Becky.

Becky pushed in the knob and hit the volume, "KKRS!"(insert your favorite rock n' roll)

Simon and Kim continued badgering each other, getting to know one another, and having just plain fun. Kim laughed when told about the indian friend Simon had as a youngster, it was actually Simon she laughed about, trying to do what the indian boy did, riding bareback and throwing long sticks shaped like javelins. Well, Simon was not one to stay on a pony very long and his sticks never went far.

The windshield started to gather raindrops, "Simon, you had to say it would rain!" Becky turned on her wipers. "Say, Pat, can we stop over at your house and change?"

"Yeah. Where else were you going to go?"

"I know, I just wanted to make sure. And it is all right if we stay with you tonight?" Becky asked.

"Yes, you can stay!"

Simon reached up and put his hand on Becky's shoulder, "I didn't say nothing about the rain, I said it might snow!"

"Uh, will you quit! I don't want no snow!" Becky looked over to Pat, "You put up with this guy?"

"Not often," Pat assured. "I only see him once in awhile."

31

Simon fell back into his seat, laughing. Kim nodded her head, not quite sure of the character next to her, and then emptied her bottle into her mouth. Pat cracked her window open just a hair, listening to the radio, as Becky drove forward, singing along.

"Well, I've sat here long enough," Irvin whispered to himself, "might as well get the cows." He put the bottle back on the shelf, walked through the barn, and opened the big door, "Go-Boss! Go-Boss!" He got behind the cows and directed them in. Somehow they just knew right where to go."

"5:30, what time does wrestling come on?" Tuck asked Burt after looking at his watch. The sport of all seasons. Some say it's not a sport, but anything carried into the Olympics has to be a sport, right?

"Hey, there we go! Channel 13." Burt acted as if a fire alarm had been set off. "Who's your favorite? Mine's that guy who, uh, what does he do?"

"I would have to go with the champ! As much shit as he's had to go through to get the belt."

"Ah, come on. Nope, I like that other guy," Burt turned his head side to side, "I just can't remember his name!" Tuck flipped through the channels. Serby's might have been a small bar in a small town, but they did carry a satellite dish—football games, pay-per-view wrestling, and late-night skin. Stopping at channel 13, "There it is! And there's my guy! Now what's his name?"

Tuck covered his mouth, hiding a laugh, and then answered the crazy-man's obsession, "Jack Lavender?"

"Yeah, Jack, that's his name! By the way, I'll take one of those!" Hand held high, Tuck knew exactly what he called for, square brown bottle from Tennessee.

Becky turned down the volume as they entered town and looked into the rearview mirror, "Simon. where do you want to go?"

"Hah?" Simon didn't quite understand the question.

"We're going over to Pat's for awhile, do you want to come with us or do you want to be dropped off somewhere?" She slowed down, almost to a stop, to be ready for Simon's request.

"Just take me up to Serb's!"

Becky had passed the turn off to Pat's, she had been hoping to lose Simon for awhile, and kept going straight up Main Street. Serby's stood a block away.

"Come on Josie, get in your stanchion!" Irvin had names for all 26 cows, at the time, no calves were in his herd. "Why can't you be more like Elvis? She's so nice and gentle, and you, ah, now get in there!" He kicked her hind quarters and she finally went forward into her stanchion. "Man, you can be something else!"

The rest of the cows, from Elvis and Whitey to Scrappy and Mother, were all in their stanchions ready for the next step, feeding time.

Becky opened her door and got out, lifting the seat forward for Simon, "Here you are!"

"Yup, here I am, good ole Serby's!" Simon straightened up, catching Becky before she got back into the car, "You're coming down, later, aren't you?"

Becky stopped and eyed his expression, was he asking for her sake or for his, "I don't know, maybe." She would have said definitely if he wasn't going to be there hitting on her.

"Oh, excuse me, not for my sake," he held his hands out then put one hand upon his chest, "but my roommate, Tuck. If you remember him?" Simon knew about Irvin and Kim and also about himself and Becky, but he wasn't quite sure if Tuck had ever met Becky or Kim.

"I don't know. Do I know, Tuck?" she looked into the car, asking openly.

"You might," Pat answered. "He's been here awhile."

"Well, then, I guess we will be back," Becky nodded as Simon stepped out of her way of getting into the car. She then sat down, shut the door, and pressed on to Pat's house. "He really is a nice guy."

"Simon?" Pat confirmed.

"Yeah," Becky acknowledged, "if we wouldn't have ended up at the lake skinny-dipping last time, I think we could be very good friends. And I don't know about you," she looked in Pat's direction, "but I could use some friends. Friends on the man side of things."

Kim caught bits and pieces, but not the whole story, "What are you talking about, the man side of things?"

32

Becky looked into her rearview mirror, "Don't you ever wonder how they see things, through their eyes? I mean, we all can't be the same."

"I hear ya." Pat sat back into her seat, using her hands as communication tools, "North and South, man and woman, black and white, far and near, and what was that book about the planets, men are from one place and women from another?"

"Yeah, okay." Kim dared herself to the top of the fence, but she wasn't about to cross over it, not yet. "So we're all human beings, but we have two distinct choices?"

"Well, it's not really a choice. I mean we are born this way," Pat lifted her breasts, "you know?"

"What about those who say they're not satisfied with who they are and get a sex change?" Kim poured on the sugar. "Are they born that way?"

"Whew! I thought you were over your identity crisis," Pat's hand to her forehead. "Just pull right in here," she motioned to Becky. They had arrived at Pat's quaint little dwelling, two bedroom, two-door garage, spacious kitchen, and fireplace. And one bathroom.

"Well, Pat, are you gonna give me an answer?"

Pat kept silent until she got out of the car and started to walk towards the house. She reached the door and held it open for her guests. Becky walked in as Kim stopped on the top step, turning towards Pat, "What if I wanted to give you a kiss?"

Pat picked up her right hand and placed her index finger upon Kim's mouth, "If you wanted to do it you would have all ready done it, so, shhh, your tired. Let's go in for awhile." Pat pushed softly upon Kim's back and followed her into the house. For Kim it had not only been a long day, coming in from Minneapolis and all, but it had been a long life. She just hadn't learned how to let go.

Simon checked out his truck before going into Serby's, no reason, he just had to open the door and look inside. He opened the glove box and noticed nothing had been moved, lifted the seat forward, noticing a cloth bag, but decided to leave it alone- all is well. He decided to reach over and lock the passenger door, he would lock the driver's side, also. "Okay," he gave himself a check, turned away from the truck, ran across the street, and into Serby's. "Hey, wrestling! It's Jack Lavender!"

Tuck raised his eyebrows, not only at the entrance, but he had never known Simon to watch wrestling. And he knew Jack Lavender? "Where are you coming from?"

"Don't matter, just pour me some orange juice!" Simon took a stool, grinning as if he had won the lottery. "Started raining!"

"What has you all jacked up?" Tuck could tell Simon was not in the same mood as he was earlier in the day. "You get laid or something?"

"Hey, leave Jack alone," Burt, totally in his buddy's epic, Jack Lavender holding the microphone and calling every ticket holder a S.O.B., mixed his hearing between wrestling commentary and Simon's afternoon. Now, who would do that?

Tuck waved Burt off as he handed Simon his orange juice, "Man, how do you know Jack?" Tuck pointed at the screen.

"I dibble and dabble, but I do pay attention to what I see, especially if I like it, which brings me back to this afternoon." Simon's happy place was worth sharing. "You missed it, Tuck!"

"Go figure. Like I didn't tell you it would be a boring day for me," Tuck spoke with exhaustion.

"I've been here!" Burt, not one to feel left out, hearing what he wanted to hear and ......

Tuck glanced back at Burt and shook his head, "You don't count. You're always here."

Simon patted Burt on the back, "Just don't take it personal."

"Hey, don't be getting privy with me," Burt slipped his shoulder down and away from Simon's reach. "I ain't telling you no personal stuff, it's, uh, it's personal!"

"Chill," Simon spoke gently, not wanting to erupt the volcano, "my hands are off." He showed his hands in a raised fashion, sitting up straight, a sign of apology and truce.

Tuck stepped in front of Burt, "You need another?"

"You know, Gracie," Irvin talked to his cows as if they were his children, maybe they were his parents, "women just bring me down. Or is it me?"

Gracie sounded her beloved feature, "Mooo!"

"Okay, I agree, it's me. So, what should I do? Should I keep trying to apologize for my wrongs with Pat, should I move on to greener pastures," Gracie's tale almost slapped Irvin in the face,

33

"Hey, sorry about that!" He padded her belly. "But what should I do? Maybe I won't do nothin' but give it time." He continued to milk and started to whistle, his answer suited him fine.

"What an afternoon, huh?" Becky tried making conversation as she looked over to Kim. No answer came, "I guess you are sleeping. Pat!"

Pat came rushing from the kitchen, where she had been mixing up some drinks, after hearing Becky's yell, "What is it?"

Becky bent over laughing, "It's not that serious."

"Well, shit, you just don't scream!"

"Oh, relax. I was just wondering what we're going to do with her," she pointed to Kim, whose head lay back with eyes closed.

"I told her she's tired," Pat knelt down to Kim's side, placed one hand on top of Kim's hand and placed her other hand upon Kim's forehead. "Let her sleep for awhile, it's still early."

"Okay," Becky listened like a five year old daughter listens to her mother. "Whatever you say."

Pat took a deep breath and exhaled, in her mind she wondered, "Are these two girls here for me or is it the other way around? Maybe both."

"Yep, you missed it Tuck," Simon pressed on, even though it seemed as though Tuck was caught up in his own depressing afternoon. "The ladies are back in town!"

Burt heard ladies and turned his ears 'on'. Tuck glanced away from the wrestling, "What ladies?"

"I don't know if you remember them, Becky and Kim from Minneapolis. They were here about two years ago."

"They grew up here!" Burt corrected forcefully. "Them girls are sweet," Burt remembered Kim and Becky very well, especially when he had his rendevous with Patty. "We had some times, I tell ya."

Tuck still remained loss about their identity, "Have I ever met them?"

"Remember when I was going out with Donna, and then we all of a sudden broke up?" Simon laid out the clues. Tuck flipped back into his memory bank, but came up blank, nodding his head. "Well, Becky, the shorter of the two, she was part of the reason."

"Don't go blaming someone else for your mistakes, buddy," Burt took very kindly to these ladies, as though they were his sisters.

"Okay, okay, I didn't mean to blame her. It was my fault," Simon shouldered his own mistakes. "But maybe you were gone that weekend, or something?" Simon couldn't figure out why Tuck hadn't known them, they moved here to Mayville at the same time and always seemed to be a day's news apart.

"Maybe I was in St. Cloud," Tuck couldn't put his finger on it, maybe it was a weekend he rather block out, "seeing my estranged wife."

"That's it!" Simon now knew and put it all together, "You were in St. Cloud seeing your wife, or rather ex-wife."

"We weren't divorced, yet!" Tuck interrupted with his version.

"Yeah, but you have never gone back."

"That doesn't mean I don't want to."

"What's stopping you? If you love somebody don't you fulfill their needs?" Simon threw arrows, Mr. Cupid sipping an orange juice in a smalltown bar.

"What's stopping me is the court system. Every time my name gets cleared I end up messin' up, again, and get the book thrown at me!" Tuck hated talking about his misfortunes, but Simon knew how much tougher it was holding them in, he had been there.

"And what's the name of this book?" Simon hoped for a bull's-eye.

"Huh? There is no name. Here, why don't you find something on cable. We've talked enough." Tuck grabbed the remote, which lay on the other side of Burt and tossed it to Simon.

"I don't want to watch anything," Simon held the remote, checking out Burt from the corner of his eye. "Besides, your customer, here, is into this fake wrestling."

"Whoa, pretty boy!" Burt disliked the comment. "You want to go a few rounds?" Burt placed his hand smack in the middle of Simon's chest, he's serious!

34

"See what you get yourself into, Simon?" Tuck seen the moment as someone, Burt, standing up for him, agreeing with him, and protecting him, but in actuality it was Simon who had the protection. It had been Simon's way of ending his conversation with Tuck, but there would be another time.

"Hey, I'm just kidding, big guy," again, Simon held his hands in sur-render mode. "There is no way I would get in the ring with one of those brutes. They'd tear me apart!" He put the remote down, "why did you hand this to me?"

"Is it all right if I take a shower?" Becky asked, standing up from her chair.

"Yeah, go ahead. I might take one myself. I need a little pick-me-up!" Pat had been zoning in on the television, clearing her mind more than anything. "It's been one of those days!" She then got up, along with her mixed drink, and walked towards the front window. Becky started walking through the kitchen, on her way outside to get a change of clothes out of the car. Kim's eyes lay motionless. "What a day indeed."

"Okay, Smokie, you're number thirteen to get your teats squeezed! Move your haunches over and give me some room." Irvin didn't like the idea of milking cows, that is, until he started. Once he started, there were times when he caught himself looking for another cow. "How's your day been, anyway? Has it been as complicated as mine?" Smokie kept munch-ing on the hay. "Yeah, you are luckier than I am."

Becky came back into the house with a duffel bag in each hand, one her's and the other one Kim's. She strolled into the living room and set Kim's bag down beside her. She noticed Pat checking out the rain, "You sure you don't want to take a shower first?"

Pat turned, her face relaxed, "No. You go right ahead."

"Are you all right?" Becky noticed the change of mood.

"Oh, yeah. I was just thinking about the past," Pat did not hide her feelings, not from her friends. "I guess I'm not so sure about me and Irvin. Is it really him I care for or is it the security he can bring to my life?"

Becky stopped from taking another step and put her bag down, "What do you mean?"

"Is it love or money? Heart or fame?" She had been thinking about how much the town knew the Baker family, which is everything. Big farmers, hard workers, town contributors, and Irvin, an only son who led the high school to getting its place on the map. State champs in football and runners-up in basketball, with Irvin in the control seat. "Am I doing anything for myself?"

Becky reached down and unzipped her bag, pulling out a pack of cigarettes, "You want one?"

"Yeah, I'll take one," Pat held out her hand in acceptance. "Sometimes life can be so difficult, but it's us that makes it that way, isn't it?"

Becky stood up, "I would have to agree with that." She lit her cigarette, kept the flame going, and lit Pat's cigarette. "Do you think guys talk about the same things we do?"

Pat inhaled, then blew out a ring of smoke, "Do we really want to know?"

"You have a point there. I'm going to the bathroom." Becky picked up her bag and strolled down the hallway. She entered the bathroom, organized her belongings, and started to undress. Once undressed she turned on the shower, testing its temperature, and stepped in, pulling the curtain beside her (insert your own feelings—an invigorating shower, or a nice bubble bath, but do not fall asleep).

Pat glided into the kitchen taking a seat at the table, wondering if she is hungry or not, "The clock says supper time, but I don't feel like eating. Must be the powder." She guided her index finger around the top of her glass, took a hit from her cigarette, and blew the smoke into the glass, putting her mind into a blank stage. She had been thinking too much.

"Okay, Simon, where are these ladies, now?" Tuck asked, the quietness getting to him, and he had had enough of the wrestling soap-opera.

"They'll be here!" Simon, always listening.

"Really! My sisters coming down here?" Burt's excitement shown brightly. He turned his head away from the television, giving his full attention to Simon. "When they coming?"

"They shouldn't be that long, but then again, you know women."

"Think I should go home and change?" Burt wants to look his best for the ladies. Simon giggled as Tuck looked at his own ensemble.

"No, you don't have to change," Simon answered. "I'm sure they rather see you just as you are."

35

"Come on, Glider, number fifteen on my list," Irvin stood in the middle of the pack, a little over halfway done. "You're so smooooth!"

"Ah, did that feel good," Becky's muscles were loosened up, no more tension, and she felt alive, again. She gently wiped herself dry, remembering a song from her high school years, "One on one I want to dance with you tonight. One on one, I do." She redressed into a black outfit, with midnight blue trim, a black mid-thigh skirt with the blue blouse, along with a blazer, which shared both colors. Her shoes put her a half-inch taller, stylish straps from the best designer in the country. This lady's business is pleasure!"

"Ah, I don't know," Burt had been fidgeting ever since wrestling had ended and Simon took control of the remote, flipping from channel to channel. "I think I will go home and change."

"Suit yourself," Simon gave no advice.

"Yeah, I'll see you guys in a bit." Burt stood up and rocked towards the door, he then looked back to see if anyone would change his mind. No one looked, so he continued to leave.

"There, now that he's gone, you want to split a pizza?" Tuck had been waiting for Burt's departure. He would've shared a pizza with him, too, but Tuck wasn't quite sure on how much Burt conveyed back to Serby.

"No problem. Do you think the clicker got to him?" Simon held up the remote.

"Probably." Tuck stood at the end of the bar, where the freezer stood, and pulled out a pizza, "Pepperoni?"

"No problem, you're the host."

Tuck unraveled the wrapper and stuck the pizza in the little oven. "So, what else you going to tell me about these women?"

"All I know is that your eyes are going to be filled! These ladies are nice," Simon said it as he seen it. "Maybe you should change your clothes."

Tuck looked down and back up at Simon, "Huh?"

"Just kidding! What you want to watch?" Again, he switched subjects on Tuck, but he only wanted the suspense to get bigger, more interesting. He wanted to hold Tuck's emotions in the palm of his hand.

"Oh, so you're gonna leave me hanging? You're not going to tell me about their features, if they wear glasses, what color of hair they have, are they married?" Tuck had his rules, no rings on the wedding finger. "Huh, are they are involved?"

Simon shrugged his shoulders, "Guess you'll have to find out."

"Okay, Patty, all's yours!" Becky strutted into the kitchen.

"Here, I made some sandwiches," Pat stood at the cupboard, then turned towards Becky, "Whoa! If you're not out to kill!"

Becky smiled and shook her hair back, "That's why I'm here!"

"Whssh," Pat's eyebrows went up. "Mayville, watch out! Is Kim still sleeping?"

"Not for long. It's time to step out!"

"I hear ya. You just made me step up! No jeans and sweatshirts, tonight."

"Nope, we gotta follow the pattern,"

"And you set quite the fold!"

"And you can follow it just fine!" Becky took her fashion seriously. Kim might have been the model, but Becky was truly the designer, and tonight, they were out to get noticed—Big Time!

"Scrappy, Scrappy, you're always dirty, but what would I do without you? You're my oldest and dearest. Others might not think much about you, but I sure do. You big old bovine!" Irvin pulled on Scrappy's ears, laughing.

"Pizza done?" Simon asked, not because of hunger, but he figured a few more minute and the pizza would be toast. Him and Tuck had found an interesting documentary on the Discover channel, something to do with wolves and their habitat. "Hey, you hear me?"

"Oh, yeah," Tuck snapped out of interest. "What you say?"

"Pizza! The pizza's gonna burn!"

"Oh, I forgot all about it!" Tuck scampered over to the oven and opened it up, pulling out the pepperoni saucer, "Perfect!"

"Wake up!" Becky shook Kim, startling her.

"What!" Kim jumped forward, "Oh, you bitch. I was sleeping so good."

36

"And is that why we came here? Now, get up and get ready."

"Yes, my majesty." Kim nodded in approval.

"I'll roll one up while you and Pat get ready."

"Where is Pat?"

"She's in the shower, but she'll be done soon. I brought your clothes in," she pointed to the bag laying on the floor next to her chair.

"You in a hurry!"

"Yes, I'm in a hurry! Come on the night is waiting!"

Kim stood up and collected her thoughts, "I was having some dream."

"I don't care about no dream, now get ready, sleepy-head!" Becky strolled around the two rooms, living room and dining room, looking for a magazine or something to empty her dope on. "Here we go!" she grabbed a small dish from the China cabinet.

"You can't use that!" Kim noticed what was in her hand.

"Why not? It's only a plate."

"Yeah, about a thousand dollar plate."

"Oh. Well, what should I use?"

"Try this." Kim had bent down and opened her bag, pulling out a magazine (insert your girlfriends favorite magazine). "It'll work." She handed it over to Becky.

"What are you doing with this in there?"

"Some people like reading, have you ever tried it?"

"Hmmph," Becky stomped back into the living room, sitting down on the couch.

"What an arrogant little piece," Kim said above whisper stage, not caring if Becky heard it or not. She then took some clothes from her bag, glided over to the front window, and waited for Pat. It was about three minutes later when she heard the bathroom door open.

"Who's next?" Pat yelled from the hallway. Kim turned from the window and sauntered towards the bathroom. "Oh, I feel much better," Pat said in recognizing Kim coming down the hall.

"Good! Because I have got to wake up," Kim still felt groggy, but a good shower would do the trick. "Am I gonna have any hot water?"

"Um," Pat didn't quite know how to answer, after a ten minute sauna, "maybe?"

Becky finished rolling up a joint and found the remote control, sat back into the couch, and scanned for MTV. Once found, playing the top ten videos of the day, she turned up the volume, stood up from the couch, and moved around the room, half dancing and half snooping around.

"Mother, your it! My last lady for the night. Well, I hope not." Irvin corrected himself, he would not let a small disagreement stand between Pat and himself. He started to get pumped up, the chores close to being done, and figured an apology would be accepted. "Mother, should I get her something special? How about flowers? Nope, the flower shop is long closed and too far away. How about a candle with an open invitation?

How's that sound?" Mother kicked her back leg upwards and swished her tail. "All ready then!"

"How's the pizza?" Tuck asked in customary fashion.

"Not bad, not bad at all, but how did you slice it up?" Some pieces were long and thin while others were short and wide.

"Sometimes I do it this way, sometimes I slice it up Chicago style, and sometimes I do it the normal way, the pie-way!" Tuck shown each technique using his hands as the cutter tool.

"You gotta slow down, man. You're too much," Simon nodded with a grin, then continued to eat. He finished off the piece he had in his hand and asked, "Did you ever do anything with your website?"

"Shh, I tried."

"What do you mean, you tried? You either made it or you didn't."

"I started one, Banana and Peach, but then I lost my password, so, I tried a second, Raven XIII, but I missed the instructions on how to activate a cover page, and now, well with this DWI and all, I just haven't been focused enough."

"Thinking about St. Cloud?" Simon, again, went for the bull's-eye.

Tuck looked up from taking his last bite, "You got it. I just can't shake it."

"You mean her, you can't forget her?"

"She's with me everyday, Simon. In one way or another she is here."

37

"Memories and horror movies!"

"What?"

"Oh, nothing. Keep eating your pizza. I've had enough, but I will take a soda," Simon switched from his ordinary orange juice. "And by the way, I have been working some overtime...."

"Yeah?"

"And I'm taking Monday and Tuesday off, maybe we can work on that website?"

"I'm game. I gotta get something better than this." Tuck waved his arm out to the side, his emphasis on the bar.

Pat marched into the living room, "What you doing?" Becky's hands were in Pat's CD collection.

"Oh!" She pulled her fingers out from between Frampton and Young. She wore the look of being caught as she turned to where the voice came from, "Pat."

"Yes and what are you doing?" Pat didn't mind, but what's wrong with some interrogation. Put Miss Arrogant and Pride on the hot seat. Ask her questions and let her sweat.

"Just looking. Is that all right?"

"Do you let anyone look at your stuff?"

"Yes. What's your problem? It is a free world!" Becky's temper lived on a short fuse.

"But this is not an open house, Missy," Pat kept her calm.

"I can't even check out your music?"

"Do I check through yours? Do I come up to your fancy apartment and start snooping around?"

"Uh, Pat, it's only CDs."

"And where else have you been looking? Did you check out my kitchen, my closets, have you been in the basement?"

"Uh, would you drop it all ready?"

Pat moved closer to Becky and put her finger in the middle of her chest, "You listen to me little Miss Pretty, we're going out to have fun tonight and you best not be acting like some school girl!"

"Excuse me?"

"In other words," Pat tapped upon Becky's chest, "I'm just bullshittin'! You can snoop around all you want, I have nothing to hide. She backed away and laughed.

"Uh, you, Patricia, Patricia." Becky shook her head.

"But don't call me, Patricia!"

"So, you're going to help me out with a website?" Tuck held back more than showing enthusiasm.

"Why not? You're not the only one who can run the 'box'!"

"I mean, what if I don't want to do it?"

"And you just said you needed something better than this bar? Why can't you accept a helping hand?" Simon seen through Tuck, he could manage a major hotel, a football team, or even a major business, but his one problem—delegation, Tuck wanted to run the whole show.

Tuck mumbled and grabbed a towel, the door opened and a few customers entered. They weren't familiar faces, yet. After a few table calls and some chatter, where-you-froms and who's-your-neighbor, the faces lost their 'stranger' label and became almost family, at least by the drinks they ordered.

Becky's fingers flipped through Pat's CDs, finally stopping with amazement, "Oh, cool! I didn't know you had this one! She pulled it out and showed it to Pat, "Can we play it?"

"Go ahead. I'm sure you know how to work a CD player."

Kim entered the living room, still feeling down, "I just can't wake up!"

"This'll help!" Becky showed her the CD cover and proceeded to activate the music.

"I hope so. I'm feeling woozy, like I could faint or something," Kim had put on extra make-up, noticing the paleness of her face, but also knew she couldn't go on hiding her sick feelings. Pat came over towards Kim.

"Have you been hiding something?" Pat stared directly into her eyes.

"I don't think so," Kim spoke the truth. She had felt nauseous the last couple days, but blamed it on the weather and her nerves.

"Maybe you shouldn't go out."

"She's going out!" Becky voiced. "We have to."

38

"I'll be okay."

The music starts and the beat picks you up. The train kept trying and finally made it over the hill. Kim put her mind on bright issues, being among friends and being back in the town she grew up in. The beat begins to move you. Do we really need the words? Becky's hips begin to swing, she raises her arms up high. Pat laughed at her funny dance. A smile grew across the face of Kim.

"And here's my best part!" Becky yelled above the rhythm. "(insert your favorite line)"!

"Three beers and a bag of pretzels," Tuck mentioned to Simon as if he cared.

"So, what's that telling you?"

"They'll be gone, shortly or they'll stay all night!"

"How about 'Red Light, Green Light'?"

"Hmm?" Tuck could never keep a straight conversation with Simon. The Game-boy was always changing context. "Now what subject are you on?"

"Website! You need a catchy name!"

"Oh. I already have one," beer glasses full and a bag of pretzels on the tray, Tuck starts to walk away, towards his customers. "Rainbow's Edge!"

"That'll work...."

"Go on, now!" Irvin kicked the last cow out the door. "A quick shower and change of clothes," he felt his chin, "don't need no shave. And I'm out of here!" He ran through the barn, shutting off the lights, and ran to the house. The rain still came down, as well as the temperature, but Saturday night—Irvin's night to show the crowd how he made his name, Magic!

Do all things appear the same to all people? Do we see the same things? Do we understand the same meanings? And how many languages to know.

When some people look at the color green they see yellow, or are we the ones seeing yellow as green? If you change from blue jeans to wearing a red dress, will your attitude differ?

We talk a good talk, but can we walk it? We smile for the camera because we're told to. When we enter into a social gathering, our personal lives are left at the door, or do they have a tendency to follow us in?

Kim perked up and joined the other two dancing in the living room, "You know this is crazy!"

"Who says? Come on and loosen up, get down, get up, get all around!" Pat is in high gear, the night time hours belonged to her. "Did anyone roll up any treats for the road?"

"I did, I did!" Becky's hand in the air, as if a third grader trying to pass the grade on being a teacher's pet, alone. "I put it right over there!" She pointed to the corner table.

"Let's smoke it, then!"

Becky ran the short distance and picked it up from under the ashtray, "Lighter, anyone?"

The ladies jammed to the music, remained doing a half-dance and passed the 'burning chalk'. The living room spills of an odor and a light fog. Eyes start to squint, red taking its color. Minds are loosing tension, fading into the music, the beat goes on and on and on. "Shall we go and spoil this town?" Pat asks openly with a grin of trouble. "I am hot, tonight.

Anyone gets in the way of this cat.....Meow!" A feline ready to attack, claws sharpened, body tight about to pounce, and the eyes, oh, the eyes!

"Short-timers." Tuck noticed the three men getting ready to leave.

Simon turned away from the television, "Yep. You're right."

"And where are these ladies? If there really is any."

"No doubt me." Simon pointed at the clock on the wall, "when the big hand lands on the four."

"Yeah. As if you know."

"And Burt? He'll be opening the door about.......right now!" The door opened and in stepped the slickest, clean-shaven, bright-clothed mechanic Tuck had ever seen.

"Whoa, Nellie, turn down the lights!" Tuck shaded his eyes. "Mr. Slick is in the house!"

Burt stepped up to the bar and leaned forward, kicking the stool out of his way, "I'll have a frosty mug and a bag of pretzels, please." Holding back the laughter takes strength.

"Okay, ladies! We walkin' or driving?" Pat did both.

"We're driving!" Becky grabbed her purse, she could no longer wait. "Let's rock this town!"

The other two ladies grabbed their purses and chased after Becky. They were feeling young, energetic, and carefree, their night to win, their night to succeed, their night to grab someone's heart. The ladies are dressed beyond '10s'. Bright colors written with want written all over them.

The night arrived, still raining a light mist, with no moon in sight and the stars tucked away in the clouds. "Remember how we used to dance under the street lights?" Kim asked, pointing at the light on the corner. "Should we go back in time?" She didn't wait, she just did it. Running under the light, spreading her arms out and wide, "And now, Ladies and Gentlemen!"

"Under the Bigtop, in the third ring!" Becky ran towards Kim, taking her place on cue. Pat waited in the shadows, until, "It's the lady in red!"

Pat takes center stage, "Let's live it up, let's give it up!" at the top of her lungs. They all bend over in laughter. "And this is when old man Prody would turn on his porch light, come outside, and yell at us to go home!"

"Oh, the days! We had great times, didn't we?" Kim at her nostalgic best.

"Yes we did, great times!" Becky looks into the light, where had the years gone, what happened to their dreams. "And when we were kids, we had the world!" She rises her arms up high.

"We still can! Let's go and show this town we're still alive!" Pat feels an adrenaline rush, with no excuse to stop it. They run up the car and jump in. Becky turns the key, hits the radio knob, turns up the volume, and pushes it into gear. A night of a thousand eyes is exactly what they want.

Irvin had taken his shower, made a quick sandwich, and dressed in his best blue jeans and denim shirt, "The shirt always gets 'em!" He ran out the house, then remembered the candle thing, so, he

40

ran back in and found a candle, putting a note, rather an invitation, around it. "One night to become as one..."

"Okay, Burt, I have a bet with you." Tuck the con-man.

"What kind of bet?" Burt plays it cool.

"Simon says the ladies show when the big hand lands on the four. You believe him?"

"Sounds a bit foolish to me," Burt takes a slow sip from his mug, puts it down, checks out Simon, turns back to Tuck, "how much?"

"Two free ones!" Tuck points at Burt's mug.

"How about two free Jack/Cokes?" Burt had it in his mind he would switch to the good stuff once the ladies showed up, make him look a little more sophisticated, a little rich and tasteful.

"Okay, I say, for those two drinks," Pointing at Mr. Slick, "Simon's correct!"

"What if I believe him?"

"You had your chance and now I take the odds! Two drinks if you win, free maintenance on my buddies truck if you lose!"

"Ah!" Burt hated betting, but he gets sucked in once again.

Simon checks out the clock on the wall, "10,9,8,7,6,5,4,3,2,1, and the door opens!" Pat steps forward, holds the door, and in come the strangers. "Welcome, ladies!"

"Hi, Simon!" Becky plays Miss Manners, if she's going to land the bartender she better be treating the guests with honor and respect. "May I take the seat next to you?"

"You sure may." Simon helps her play the part, a regular Rhett Butler to Scarlet O'Hare. Simon stands and pulls out the adjoining stool, "Here you are and my I introduce you to the guys?" He fans his arm to show recognition, "Burt and Tuck, from there I'll let them tell the story."

Becky ate it up, going along with the invisible script, "And I am Becky, for now."

"Nice to meet you," Tuck beats Burt to her hand, which lay on the bar. "And my I?" After she nods Tuck gently picks up her hand and melts his lips on her fingers.

"Thank you," a blush and a blink.

"Hey, you know me, right?" Burt steps in, awkwardly.

"Is that you, Burt?" She keeps with the sweetness, putting her melting eyes into Burt.

"Yeah, how have you been?"

"Fine and getting even finer," she turns back to Tuck. "Could we have some drinks, please?"

Pat and Kim kept their distance, they know who handles the guys. After hearing Becky ask for drinks they move towards Burt, "Hi, Burt!"

Burt turns to his side, "Hi, Patty! You like my shirt?"

"You look just fine, Honey," Pat pinches his cheek, turning it a blush-red. "You buying tonight?"

"Oh, yeah, I'm buying! Mr. Bartender these ladies are thirsty!" Isn't it funny, once someone special walks in you're only a bartender? "Um, what'll it be Patty and Kim?" Burt digs out his wallet and begins to leaf through the bills, pictures, business cards, and stuff. He grabs the bills and puts them on the bar, "Hell, as far as I'm concerned you ladies can spend it all!"

"Sugar Daddy!" Kim smiles and shoulders next to Burt. "In that case pour me the House Special!"

"Make it two!" Pat chimes in.

"Oh, we forgetting someone?" Becky makes herself look important. Turns to Tuck, "That'll be three, please." She puts her hand on Burt's arm, "Thank you kindly, my dear old friend."

Burt heats up, Simon sits back and enjoys the scene, "And the House Special!" Tuck checks out the racks and bottles, glasses and colors, "will be...." he turns to the ladies, wearing red, blue, black, and green, "a Margarita here," He singles out Kim, "Strawberry Daiquiri to the lady in red," which is Pat, "and for the lady in front a Raspberry Kami!"

"A Raspberry ....." she questions.

"I'll make it a special one. You'll like it." Tuck just above a whisper, making points.

Simon nodded his head noticing the demeanor and presence of peace in Tuck's delivery. Burt continued to sweat, counting the bills in front of him and trying to act like he's in control. He lays down a five dollar bill. Tuck sees the five-spot and gets Burt's attention. Burt senses the language and lays down another five.

"Place hasn't changed much," Kim eyes the place over.

41

"You weren't here that long ago!" Pat excuses the small-town pace.

"I guess not. Say, Burt, remember how we used to kick your ass in pool?" She hits him on the shoulder, teasingly.

"Not always!" A man and his competitive nature. "I could beat you now!" He stood straight, sucking in his stomach, rubbing his fingernails up and down his shirt buttons. "I pretty good." He blows on his nails. Mr. Slick.

"I'm just kidding, Burt," Kim smiles. "Oh, you can be so cute!"

"Cute! I don't want to be cute," Burt and his mug meet at his mouth. He finishes it and bangs it down on the bar, "I'll have one of those, uh, fancy drinks!" Jack almost slips out of his mouth, but he has to keep up with what the ladies are drinking. It is his money they're spending.

Tuck empties the blender and hands the Strawberry Daiquiri to Pat, "and a couple of these," he throws in three filberts. "And since I made enough," he lifts another glass, fills it , and hands it to Burt, "here's one for you, a fancy drink."

"Thanks," Burt's face is a light reflection of the drink in front of him. How the bartender can teach us things without even knowing it, or do they do it on purpose?

Tuck grabs the clear square bottle with a yellow label, pours it into the blender, grabs a couple handfuls of ice, "It's all in the ice!" noticing a few observers. He mixes in the other ingredients and pushes the button 'liquefy'.

"Margarita!"

"Is that what this is?"

"No, Burt, you have a Daiquiri. Just like Pat," Kim confirmed. "Can I have a taste?"

"Sure. It's pretty good." He lifts the glass allowing her to put her lips on the straw and suck in. "Pretty good, huh?"

"Mmm, it's real good!" flirtation eyes.

"And the Margarita lands here!" Tuck places the glass down gently. And now for the Raspberry.

Irvin jumps into the truck, turns the key, and maneuvers himself off the yard, "Saturday Night, Saturday Night, S-A-T-U-R-D-A-Y Night!" A British band fills his vocals. He heads out of the driveway and onto the gravel road. Seven miles in five minutes, he's done it before. He's by Pete and Donna's already and looking for his left turn. "Here I come!" He sees the left turn, slows down, turns into it, and pushes down, Mayville lay straight ahead.

The rain stops momentarily, but the temperature continues to fall. The roads are slippery, but manageable. As long as you watch how you're driving. There's also been deer spotted on this stretch of road, but with the rain and all, they're probably hiding out by the lake amongst the trees.

Irvin reaches over and opens his glove box, "I need some tunes," he flips through some cassettes, 'why change to CDs when I have all these tapes?' finally settling on an old favorite. "Here we go. I think it's Pat's favorite." He shoves the tape into the cassette player and it jams-up, "shit!" He looks down trying to pull the tape out, he notices headlights coming at him from a distance, bright lights shining. "Man, turn off the high beams!" The tape comes loose and falls to the floor, instinctively he reaches for it, his hand on the steering wheel swerves the vehicle in the direction of his body, hits loose gravel. Irvin notices the pull and quickly reacts. He places both hands on the steering wheel, turning the truck away from the ditch. The headlights in front of him are now very close. He swerves back toward the ditch, trying to maintain control. The headlights are almost on top of him, a blaring noise comes from the other vehicle, he slammed on the horn!

"Whew! Too close," Irvin wipes his forehead, takes a deep breath, blinks his eyes. "Okay, everything is okay." He leaves the cassette on the floor and turns on the radio.

"Mmmm, this is different," said in a sweet voice. Becky takes another taste of the milkshake-like beverage. "What's in this?"

Tuck waves his finger in front of her, "Bartender's secret."

Becky leans forward, "Do you have any more you would like to share?"

Tuck leans forward, within an inch of her nose, "I'm working."

"And I'm dressed for business," she leans back showing her attire.

"You're good," Tuck straightens up and gives a grin filled with style.

"So, they tell me."

"Tuck! Can I get some quarters, please?" Simon interrupts.

42

"Yeah, no problem," he gets the quarters, keeping a watchful eye on the beauty before him. Tuck's had a few dates and short-term relationships since leaving his wife and the city behind him, but something or some feeling had always pulled him away, or pulled him back. Maybe things would change, tonight!

Simon held his hand out as Tuck dropped the coins, "I've got just the right thing." He strolls over to the jukebox and inserts the coins, Kim steps up beside him, "Hi," his head turns towards her, "you sure look nice."

"Thank you, Simon. I want to tell you how much I enjoyed your company today."

"Thanks, I had fun, too," he pushes on 2323. "You want to play some tunes?"

"Okay," she pushes on 1272, checks out the screen and pushes on 2981, "I'll let you finish them off." She remains by his side, checking out his choices. Do they have anything to do with the character next to her or is he just pushing buttons? It's a gamble, but she's banking on the personality. He pushes 2499.

"You shoot darts?" He keeps her interest.

"Sometime, but I'm not that good," she keeps him going.

Pat and Burt admired their fancy drinks, occasional smiles, and short cliché's about tonight's history and future. "Remember how we used to take care of you?" She twists her head in Burt's direction.

"I used to take care of you!"

"No, no, no! Burt, you can't take care of yourself!"

"Tuck?" Becky whispers to a listening statue admiring the television, or is it his ex-wife he sees.

"Mr. Bartender?" she repeats.

"Oh, I'm sorry. Just a little lost."

"But I can see you. And by my vision you're looking really good."

"Uh, thanks. So, may I help you?"

"Well, we didn't come in here for just one drink," she lifts her empty glass. Tuck takes the glass from her, touching hands. "And we didn't come here just for drinks, either." Spoken softly, her eyes sparkling and sincere, "If you want to talk, I'm here." She sensed fear and hurt, this man had been to a place he did not want to return to. She could see a broken heart.

"Tuck we need some darts!" Simon exclaimed. "Anyone else want to play?"

"Burt you want to take them on?" Pat asked.

"Sure, I'll play."

"What game we playing, 301 or Cricket?" Simon set the rules.

"Burt?" Pat wants the man taking the lead.

"301's cool!"

"301 it is." He had already put the quarters in and motioned to Kim the appropriate game. He waited for Tuck to hand him the darts.

"Here's your Kami, and who's paying for this one?" Tuck handed Becky the glass.

"I'll get it," Simon obliged. "Got my darts?"

Tuck takes the money from Simon, gives him back the change along with six darts, "Don't beat 'em too bad." While Tuck bartends Simon had been practicing on the dart board.

"Come on, you think I'm going to let myself win?" Simon played fair, but he thought it best for everybody to win once in awhile. Although, he did expect your best. Be it darts, pool, backgammon, or on the job Simon expected fair play and an honest effort from those involved. It's how he positioned himself at the assembly plant in which he not only got on day shift, but also became assistant supervisor. Tuck sometimes misread it as ass-kissing or being a con-artist.

Pat and Burt walked over to the table occupied by Kim, "Are you any good?" Pat asking Kim, making sure she wasn't the only left-hander.

"I used to be, but it has been awhile."

Simon set the darts on the table, "Guys against girls or mixed couples?"

"Mixed couples. Me and Burt against you two."

"Sounds good. You want to go first or should we?"

"You go first." Pat slides the darts to Kim.

"Okay! Here we go Simon." Kim had once earned a trip to Chicago while playing with a bar league in St. Paul, 'Hackett's Heroes'. They finished second in state, qualifying for the trip to the

43

windy city, but once they arrived in Chicago it turned out to be one big party and a tenth place finish. "Going for the hat-trick!" Three bulls in one throw.

"Well, you want to talk?" Becky has Tuck all to herself.

Tuck turns the television to a sports channel, turns the volume down, and then turns to the volume control switch for the jukebox, "How loud we want it?" He turns the knob to 9 and his patrons respond by joining in on the song. (insert your favorite Pop song) "And what do you want to talk about?" He leans towards Becky, brown eyes in reflection mode.

Irvin hops out of his truck, undecided about the candle. He has it in his hand, throws it back in the truck, reaches for it, and then leaves it, "I'll wait until I get her alone." A light rain starts and he runs into Serby's. "Hey, guys!"

Pat stands still, noticing the door opening and the voice that follows. "My turn?" She questions Kim, who hit two bulls-eyes, but fell short on the last dart with a 19. Pat avoids the guy who just walked in, trying to focus on herself and the possibility of changing her lifestyle. She takes the darts from Kim. "Okay, Burt, wish me luck."

Irvin notices the cold shoulder and takes a place at the bar, "Tuck, what should I start with, Jack, Captain, or the big Turkey?" At least he can impress her with his alcoholic choices. "And you can also fill everyone's glasses, on me." He pulls a stack of cash from his pocket and lays it on the bar, making sure he's being noticed. "How's Becky? You sure are lookin' good!" He goes right for the hit.

"Thanks, Irvin, but you're looking in the wrong direction. Pat's over there," she points to Pat, who's eyeing up a triple 19 with her last dart. "Don't you think you owe her something?"

"I'm buying her a drink right now!"

"Oh, that'll do it."

"Hey, I've got something in the truck. I'm just saving it for later when we're alone."

"As if you're going to get her alone." Becky turned to check out the participants at the dart board. "Can't you see she's having fun without you?"

"Here, Irvin. You want to make the delivery or should I?" Tuck politely asks serving up drinks for the house. Becky slides the Kami towards herself. "Okay, one down. Now, you gonna take the rest?" he questions Irvin, who's not quite sure on how to handle the situation.

"Uh, yeah, I can handle it." Irvin gets up from his stool, Tuck hands him a tray, puts the drinks on the flat disc, and focuses on his destination. "I hope I don't spill!" He makes it to the table and sets down the tray, "Here you go! This rounds on me."

"Thanks, Irvin," Burt offers his gratitude.

Pat and Kim look at each other, another boy-ploy—buying their way into your heart. "Oh, well, thanks Mr. Baker," Pat succumbs, but by greeting him as if he were a stranger or just another neighbor down the street. She handed the darts to Simon and finished off her first drink. "You want to take this back to the bar for me?" she hands the glass to Irvin.

Irvin takes the glass, "Uh, can I talk to you in private?"

"Not now. Can't you see I'm in the middle of a game?" She turns her back to Irvin and checks out Simon's score, 33 with one dart remaining, "Miss, Simon!" The dart leaves his finger tips and lands directly in the bullseye.

"All right! Way to go, partner!" Kim jumps up and shares a high-five with Simon.

"Now, as you were saying?" Tuck leans forward in front of Becky. "You want to hear some secrets or do you just want to share stories?" His eyes still showing reflection.

"Bedtime stories or fairytales?" Becky keeps moving the mercury up.

"Say, Tuck, she won't talk to me." Irvin, no one's paying him any attention so he becomes Mr. Third-party, an annoyance. And who better to bother than the bartender.

"Who won't talk to you?" A bartender's job consists of listening, so, Tuck turned his attention to the lost soul. "Burt?" Becky laughed at the remark.

"No, not Burt! I'm talking about Pat," he lowers his voice not wanting Pat to hear. "What she I do? I don't want to beg."

"First of all, what so important about talking to Pat?"

"Well, we've been going out and now she don't want to talk."

"You and Pat. You two have been going out, and for how long?"

"Years! But now she don't want me around."

44

"And does anyone know this, that you two been going out?"

"Well, yeah, can't you tell?"

"Let me see, I see you hitting on any strange chick that walks in here, I see you hitting on chicks when we've been out of town, I know you go to strip bars in Minneapolis and that other town, and you know, Irvin, I never see you and Pat together. Now, tell me, again, how long have you two been going out?"

"Yeah, Irvin, tell us. Tell him what you did today!" Becky casts her two cents.

"Hey, what am I supposed to do?"

"Exactly," Tuck hangs his head. He then raises it and looks deeply into Irvin's eyes, "Do you think or do you just jump forward?"

"Hey, I think!"

"What do you think about? Do you have any idea on how to treat a woman?"

"Oh, and you're the one with the divorce, right?" Irvin pins the tail on the donkey.

"Okay, I am not here to give advice, but here's a lady, maybe she'll tell you," Tuck slides the buck, delegates his authority, suggests a reliable resource. "Becky, would you do us the honor?"

"Certainly not! The guys a pig!" Irvin slides down the bar, now elbow to elbow with Becky.

"And you're not. Who came on to who?"

Tuck takes a step back, "You two have met?"

Irvin lifts his head towards Tuck, "Oh yeah, we met all right. She show you any of her moves, yet!"

"I'm out of this," Tuck has his reasons for being single and unattached, especially when everyone seems to be involved with someone and you're only there to play safety net. Not to mention having known friends that got caught with wives—and ending up going to their funerals. "I stay out of games!" He walks from behind the bar and goes over to the dart board. "Who's winning?"

"They are!" Kim points at Pat and Burt. "But I think they're cheating!"

"Are not!" Pat hears the accusation.

"Do we need any drinks over here?" Tuck plays waiter, also.

"I guess I could go for one," Burt lifts his glass and empties it.

"Anyone else?" Tuck finds it customary to always ask twice.

"No, we're fine," Pat answers after noticing Kim's and Simon's glasses at least half full. "How's the company?" Her eyes aim at Becky and Irvin.

Tuck shakes his head, "Were you two going out?"

"Not anymore, why? You have something to tell me?" Pat smiles.

"Has Burt been talking?"

Pat puts her hand on Burt's shoulder, "I don't know. Burt, have you been talking?"

"Uh, earlier, me and Tuck."

"Oh, and what was that all about? You weren't talking about me, were you?" At this point she's hoping they were.

"Just a little," Burt ignores Tuck's facial language and admits the secret. Tuck starts to walk away.

"Hold it right there! Don't be leaving when the talk is getting good," Pat demanded.

"Your turn, Burt!" Simon hands the darts over. "Two 16s and you're out!"

Burt takes his place behind the white strip on the floor, rubs his first dart three times along the outside of his leg. He lifts his arm and pretends to aim. The dart leaves his hand as he swings forward, "There's one!" The dart lands squarely inside the 16.

"Tuck, what were you all talking about?" Pat resumes. Kim and Simon each take a drink from their respective glasses and watch Burt's next throw. "Did he mention me and Irvin?"

"Yeah, sort of." Tuck gives the simplest answer. The door opens and a few more customers walk in. "Sorry, I got customers. Maybe we'll talk sometime." He strolls back behind the bar and gets ready for customer satisfaction. The outsiders each take a stool at the bar, belly-up! "What can I get you, tonight?"

Becky and Irvin continued their small talk. He goes from Pat, and how he first knew her in high school, but being four years younger than her he figured his chances were too slim to pursue anything, to when he graduated from high school and instead of going to college on an athletic scholarship opted to join the Air Force, what a mistake. "I never wanted to join, anyway!"

45

"So, why did you?"

"A way to get out of this town, I guess."

"I don't buy that. You join the Air Force to get away and then you come back never to leave?"

"I might leave!"

Tuck sticks his nose in, overhearing Irvin, "When?"

"Hey, this isn't about you! Serve your drinks!" Becky takes a sip and thoroughly tastes it.

"Have you ever tried one of these?" She asks Irvin.

"What is it?"

"A Raspberry Kami! It's really good," her eyes wander towards Tuck.

"Hey, you looking at him?" Irvin's noticeable jealousy.

"Yeah, and it's a nice view." She licks her lips and catches Tuck's eyes making a quick glance. "You think it's a nice view?"

"You're crazy! All you women are crazy!" Irvin can't help but to turn around and watch Pat, hoping she heard his remark. Pat hesitates, but stops herself from looking. Kim misses the 18, the game-winner and pulls out the darts.

"All right, Burt, we're still in it!"

Tuck hands over three tap beers, "That'll be $3.00! Can I get you anything else?"

"Nope, but how about turning on the Timberwolves? I think they're playing Miami!"

Tuck picks up the remote, flips through the channels, "There it is! Wonder what the score is?"

"Becky?" Irvin puts his hand on her back and whispers into her ear, "did you have anymore snow?"

Becky jumps away, "Shh, don't be telling everyone."

Irvin peeks around, "I'll pay you for some. I know right where we could go and split it up."

"What if I don't want to split it?"

Irvin shrugs his shoulder, "Nothing I can do, but, come on, I had a rough day." His eyes wonder back to Pat. In his mind, "Maybe if I make her jealous she'll realize what she's missing out on."

"Number one, you either break up, completely, with her," Becky notices the glances, "or you stay far away from me." She grabs her purse and pulls out a pack of cigarettes.

"You smoke?"

"Sometime. Is that a problem?" She sets her purse down and takes a cigarette from the pack, puts it to her mouth and lights it. "Maybe you should try it before you start knocking it!"

"No thanks, I had my days." Up to two packs a day in Air Force fatigues, there was nothing better to do. Just smoke those cigarettes and play cards. "So, you want to do that?"

"Buy me a drink first. And not one of these."

"Okay. Tuck, we need some drinks here!"

"Same?"

"No. I'll have the same, but she wants.."

"You guess," she throws her eyes at Irvin.

"Um, Captain Morgan and Coke." Irvin doesn't ask he just looks at Tuck and orders.

"Good guess," she smiles while taking another drag off her cigarette.

Irvin prides himself on his guess, not knowing the trick is on him. She would have taken anything.

Now, into their second game, switching partners, Pat toed the white stripe, "Should I go for the double 18 or the 16?" she asks her partner, Kim, being they're playing Cricket.

"We have time. Just go for the 16 and we can come back to the 18s."

"Who's cheating, now?" Simon small-talking.

Pat ignores the comment and buries a double 16, "Points! We made some points!" She grabs the darts from the board and hands them to Burt, "Think you can catch us?" He returns no words and steps to the line, forty points behind and three numbers open.

Simon notices the almost empty glasses, "You ladies need another?" He might not drink, but as long as you can control your intake, Simon sees no problem in alcohol consumption.

"Sure, you buying?" Pat looks at her glass.

"Yep! I can get this one. Burt, you need one?"

Eyeing up his second dart after the first one missed its target, "Yeah. Make it a double!"

46

Simon struts to the bar and takes a seat next to Becky. "Tuck, you're messing up. We have some drinks to be delivered." He looks over his shoulder at the dart players.

"The game's on!"

Simon leans forward, without noticing the television, "Which game you interested in?"

Tuck shakes his head, "Leave me out! Now, what are you drinking?"

"Bartender, we need three more beers!" comes an order from the sports fans. "'Wolves up by five!"

Kim shoots three darts, one bounces onto the floor, one hits a bullseye, and the third darts hits a two, "I can't get the 18! Damn-it!" She yanks the darts out of the board and finds the other on the floor, "Who's next?"

"Simon! I'll get him," Pat's opportunity to ease her conscious, 'what's Irvin and Backy talking about'? She walks toward Simon, darts in hand, and approaches him on the other side, away from Becky, "Your turn, Wizard!"

Becky catches the nickname, "Wizard?"

Simon shrugs, "I don't know, maybe it's the spells I cast. Thanks for the drinks, Tuck." He leaves a dollar tip, slides one drink in Pat's direction, and picks up the other three.

"Here, I can take them," Pat helps out, wanting it to look like her and Simon might have something together. She raises her eyes to check out Irvin's reaction. He's watching, but remains silent. Pat and Simon walk back to the game. "Time for some more tunes! Who's chipping in?"

Burt lays down a buck, Simon follows, and Kim picks them up, "Here you go! Need any help?"

"I can get it, unless..." Pat backs up, not meaning to be rude.

"That's okay. Just yell if you can't find anything." Kim reads into Pat's move. She's been noticing Pat taking peeks at Irvin ever since he walked in, especially when he sat next to Becky. It's the song thing. (insert a song you share with someone special)

THE MILLION DOLLAR QUESTION 9/47

Walking down the street one day you come across a penny, not a shiny new one, not an old one dating to World War I, neither, just a penny.

You take the penny and hand it to a child, maybe you toss it into the street for someone else to pick up. Nevertheless, your luck changes.

Within two days you enter a sweepstakes, giving away multiple prizes, you enter a meat drawing at your favorite watering-hole and win three big steaks and some crab meat, and today you enter the state lottery.

Luck is going your way, and it's good luck! Now, say you win the multi-million dollar lottery, are you ready? How much will it take to become yourself?

The numbers are punched, 2222, easy to remember, maybe it's planned that way. The song begins, Pat remains studying the other selections, wondering if a shadow will appear. Does he remember the dreams they once shared, the stories they told each other. Is he in it for love and promises, or does he prefer to play the games of hide and seek?

Irvin recognizes the song, while sipping from his glass. His eyes open as his favorite verse arrives, the one when he first kissed Pat, the verse that gives their relationship meaning. All said in so few words. He lowers his glass, slowly, and turns toward the music. He pauses all actions, is he ready to go back?

"Irvin?" Becky taps on his shoulder. "Did you still want to split up some rocks?"

He shakes the memories and turns to the present, "Uh, sure. We can do it right back there." He points to the narrow hallway leading to the back exit. "My uncle's office is back there."

"Your uncle's office? You mean your uncle owns this place?"

"Yeah, Mike Serby, he's my uncle." The song plays in the distance. "You want to chop some up?" They get up from their stools, and without looking around, walk to the office. Pat catches them leave out of the corner of her eye.

"Kim!" She yells, "I need your help." Irvin still does not look back. Kim walks over to Pat and the jukebox. "Sorry, Patty. I guess you have to let go."

"You're right, but I didn't think Becky would do this to me." Pat pushes buttons at random, using up her remaining selections. "A song is just a song. Let's play some more darts." They walk back over to Burt and Simon. "My turn?"

"Yep," Simon answers. "You only need one bullseye to win." Pat picks up the darts from the table, toes the white stripe, positions her first dart, and throws—Bullseye! "We win!"

"So, what kind of price you figure on?" Becky sells she doesn't give.

"I thought, maybe, we could start over." Irvin sitting in his uncle's chair behind the desk, feels important and on-top. "What do you say?"

Becky, sitting on a folding chair next to the wall, feels cold. "Here, I'll just give you some. You have anywhere to put it?"

"Right up my nose!"

"I don't believe you! I swear you were somebody else just a second ago."

"The guy who wants to make out or the guy who wants to party!"

"No, the guy who still felt something for his girlfriend." Becky knew Pat's selection had something to do with Irvin, and now regretted being in the back office with him.

"Uh, come on. We had our time." Irvin opens the top left drawer and pulls out a mirror, complete with chopping utensils. "Now, shall we cut some up?"

"You want to play another or should we do something else?" Pat asked openly chucking her last two darts into the board. "We could go smoke a little."

"I'm for it!" Burt steps forward. "We can go down to my place."

"Sounds cool to me. Simon want to come along?" Kim approved of getting out of the bar for awhile. Pat needed some fresh air and to get away of from the scene Irvin and Becky were creating. She asked Simon knowing he rather not smoke, but you never know, he could change his mind.

"Thanks, but I'll pass. Maybe later." Simon picked up the glasses and started towards the bar. The others put on their jackets and headed out the door.

48

"We'll see you later, Tuck!" Pat and Kim wave. Tuck looks away from his customers and the sport-talk, nodding accordingly. The two ladies and the town mechanic take their first steps out the door and the wind-chill hits them, "Brrr! Is it getting cold!"

"And it's beginning to snow, just like Simon said it would!" Kim smiles while trying to catch the flakes upon her tongue.

"I should have never worn this dress, it's cold out here!" Pat wraps her arms around herself. "Are we walking or did you drive your car?"

"I always walk." Burt put his arm around Pat, "I'll keep you warm. Remember when I used to do?"

"Thanks, Burt. Whatever happened to those days?"

Burt swallows, "Your mom." They begin to walk, two and one half blocks, to Burt's domain.

"You cutting up nice lines?"

Becky had moved her chair close to the desk, but kept her distance from the wolf in sheep's clothing, "You get what you get."

"Ooo! Sounds like punishment."

"Yeah, maybe you should be getting your ass slapped." Becky straightens out the white lines. "You have a straw?" Irvin pulls one from the drawer.

"Here you go, darling!"

"Don't be calling me darling! I'm only in here to get you high."

"Sort of like having sex?"

"No! I'm going to do my line first and then you can do whatever you want with yours. And I'm getting out of here." She puts the straw to the line and inhales. "Here, I'll see you later."

"Just wait! I'm sorry for the way I'm acting. Okay? Can you just wait?" She does as Irvin takes his turn on the tooter. "Good stuff! Could you imagine if you had a million dollars?" He sits back in the chair.

"Whatever," Becky gets up from her chair, "let's go back out there." She points to the bar area.

"Wait, I want to show you one more thing. You have to come outside with me."

"Huh? It's getting cold out there!"

"It's just a few steps from here. Come on." He takes her arm and she follows. They go out the back door, down the three steps, and hook a left. "It's right over here. My uncle sort of gave it to me." He lets go of her arm and kneels down beside the building, lifting up a rock.

"What is it? I'm getting cold!"

"Maybe I shouldn't show you." He places the rock back on top of a small metal container.

"You are such an ass! Bringing me out here in the snow, umph, I'm going in!" She turns and strokes the steps, opens the door, and keeps walking until she reaches her bar stool. "What an asshole!"

"Pardon." Simon is sitting down a few stools. He watched her come in.

"That Irvin guy! What a jerk!"

"And do you know what your friends are thinking?"

Becky turns to the dart board, "Where are they?"

"They went over to Burt's place. Pat wanted to burn one."

"Uh, and I'm stuck here!"

"He lives right down the street. Why don't you just go over there?"

"Yeah, and get my ass kicked!" She takes a drink from her glass, emptying it. "How about buying me another drink instead?"

"You didn't do anything wrong, did you? So, why not just go over there?"

"Fine, Simon! If you want to get rid of me I'll just leave!" Becky jumps from her stool and starts to walk. "And if I get killed it's all your fault!"

"You won't get killed! By the way, Burt still lives in the same house, right at the end of Main Street." He points her in the general direction then turns his head to the television, "Hmph, end of the third quarter and their down by eight. I'll have to do something about this."

Becky opens the door and feels the chills. She puts it out of her mind and starts to focus on what she's going to tell Pat, "We didn't do anything—Oh yeah, like she'll believe me. Well, that's all I got. It is the truth." She picks up her pace, gets ready to cross the street, looking in both directions,

49

when, from behind her someone grabs her shoulders! "Ahhh! Who is it?" The figure puts their hands over her eyes.

"Be still and you won't get hurt. Do you understand?" The voice was not familiar. The figure takes his one hand away, the other hand covers both eyes, and pushes her into the alley. "Come on, Bitch!" She obeys the commands. The figure pushes her into the darkness and before she can turn around the figure is gone. She shakes her head and collects herself.

"What the f— was that about? I've been doing too many drugs!" She peeks out from the alley and continues on her way. "That was very strange!"

Burt opens the door to his shelter and holds it open for the two ladies. "Thanks, Burt. Oh, it's getting cold. You have the heater on?"

"Yeah, my heater is still on. I knew it would still be getting cold. You gotta give it at least until the end of April. You going to stay long or should we just smoke one?"

"I don't know, what do you think, Kim?"

"We can stay awhile. Do you have any tunes?"

"Oh yeah, there's my collection." Burt takes pride in his music, cassettes from the rock 'n' roll decades. "I have Bob Dylan, Tom Petty, Bob Seger, Wallflowers, and Scorpions. What you want to hear?"

"How about Sammy?" Pat suggests the Red Rocker.

"Yep! Which one?" Burt points in the Sammy Hagar area of the rack.

Pat bends over and pulls out one of his first, "Remember this one?"

"Good times! Three Lock Box! "Here," Burt hits the power button, "put it in!"

Kim takes a seat on the couch, "I'm glad I didn't wear a dress." She shivers and decides to keep her jacket on. "Nice place you have." The comment gets lost in the volume.

"All right! I'm sure glad you guys came over." Burt struts into the kitchen and comes back with a plate, "Who wants to roll?"

Pat sat on the couch next to Kim, "I'll do it! You have any papers?"

"So, Simon, where'd they all go?" Tuck asking his informant, while he refills three taps.

"They all went to Burt's." He puts his index finger and thumb together, then puts them to his lips, "you know?"

"Smoking! I didn't know Burt did that."

"We probably don't know a lot of what he does. But maybe that's a good thing." Simon just sits back waiting for the commercial to be over, "you think the 'Wolves have a chance?"

"They can do it."

"I say they will do it!" The front door opens and in walks two couples, followed by a pack of four women. "We have company!" He observes their actions and sitting arrangements, just a habit.

"Say, what happened to Irvin?" Tuck registers a missing body.

"He's," Simon looks over his shoulder into the hallway, "right there."

"You freak me out sometime." Tuck nods his head in honesty.

"Hey, I freak myself out." Simon leans forward, the commercial is over and the ball is put into play. Irvin sits down next to him, remains silent and fidgety. "Good powder?" Irvin does not answer, feeling somewhat uncovered and paranoid.

Becky arrives at Burt's front step and knocks. Two knocks, she hears voices, and waits for the door to open. Burt struts to the entrance and opens the door, "And what do we have here, Miss Becky!" Pat almost dumps the tray, but refrains herself. Kim waits for an explanation. Becky stands, waiting for an invitation. "Oh, I'm sorry, come on in. Where's your buddy?" He couldn't resist.

Pat repeats the question in her own fashion, "So, you little bitch, what did you all do this time?"

Becky shuts her eyes, takes a deep breath, and follows her script, "we didn't do anything. Wait, we did do something. We each did a line of coke, and that's all."

"He had some coke, huh?" Burt becomes inspector.

"No, I do. And then he took me outside to show me something. May I sit down?"

"Yeah, you can sit in that chair." Burt points to the old rocker between the corner table, holding an antique lamp, and the front door. "And I'm going to sit in this one!" He prides himself on the recliner, stuck directly in the middle of the wall with his stereo to his left along with the television. "The best seat in town!"

50

"And what was outside?" Pat gets back to the story. Becky takes a seat, dropping her purse beside her. Kim widens her listening ability.

"He wouldn't show me, said it was something his uncle gave him. I don't know. I think he's a big jerk!" Her eyes aimed directly at Pat. "What do you see in him?"

"Gotta be the money!" Kim jumps forward.

"And what else, Patricia?" Burt knows the secret, but he wants Pat to admit it. Right in front of her best friends. "Should I take a guess?" Pat sees the truth in Burt's expression.

"How do you know?" She questions upon speculation.

"Let's just say it's a small town and his uncle is my best friend. You want me to guess?"

"No. I don't like it when people are wrong. So, why don't I just roll this up and we can all drop the subject." Pat empties her baggy onto the plate and starts to clean the greenery. "Becky, my apologies."

Tuck steps back behind the bar after delivering four bottles of beer to one table and taking an order of variety from another. "Hey, Irvin, what's up?"

"Just a Captain."

"Okay, I'll get it to you after I get these folks. A Rum/Coke, plain Pepsi, and two beers," he says while picking out the bottles. So, what's up with the game?"

"Close, "Wolves are still down by a couple." Simon's eyes are glued to the action.

"They'll do it. Well, I have to deliver these and I'll be right back." Tuck slams his hand down on the bar in front of Irvin, "Hey, you okay?"

"Uh, yeah. I'm okay." Irvin looks around the room, then focuses on the television. The front door opens and in walks Bob. "Hey, Simon, it's your twin."

Simon hears Irvin, but ignores his remark. The game is on the line with fifteen seconds remaining and the 'Wolves have the ball at half-court, down by one. "Come on T-wolves." He softly demands. The guard brings it across the center line and passes it off to the shooting-guard, he fakes the shot, causing the defender to jump, and dribbles to the middle, posting up from the free-throw line. He puts it up! The ball hits the backboard and bounces off the front of the rim, rebound goes to the T-wolves. He fakes, he shakes, and he slams the rock home. "All right! 'Wolves win it!" Simon's arms are extended upward.

Tuck comes back around the bar, "They done it, huh?" He walks down to the three tap beers, "And I'll collect on my bet, please." They each hand over a dollar bill and decide it's time to go. "Thanks for your company, see you again!" He tucks the bills into his pocket and strolls over to the new guy, Bob. "What can I help you with?"

"A glass of water will be fine." He remains standing.

"Here, smoke it!" Pat tosses the reefer to Burt. "You're the host." Her way of telling him to keep his secrets untold. She brushes the weed back into her baggy, stuffs it into her purse, and puts the plate on the floor. Burt hands the stick to Becky after a long inhale.

"Where's Irvin, now?" Kim gets a suspicion bug. Becky inhales and passes her the joint. "Just curious." Becky blows the smoke at Kim.

"Leave it alone. I have no idea where the maniac is."

Kim takes a hit from the joint and passes it to Pat. The ritual continues, the fog lingers in the air, the music throbs into each person's temples. "Burt, what kind of lamp is that?" Pat asks, pointing to the figure in the corner. "Did you get it from a dead gypsy or what?"

Burt leans forward, checks out the lamp, and answers to Pat, "I got it from your mom so as to leave you alone!" What webs we weave....

"You went out with, Burt?" Becky coughs from the inhalation, or was it Burt's answer.

"You remember! When I was in eighth grade." Pat clears the past.

"If you call that going out!" Kim judges the arrangement.

"What would you call it?"

"Eer," Kim holds in the smoke and hands the joint to Pat. "I call it baby-sitting!" Becky and Burt bust out a laugh. Kim begins to cough, laugh, cough, cry. "Oh, my!" Pat holds the joint in her hand, shaking her head.

"You, you, what can I say?" She takes a hit and teases Burt with the joint, "You want it, no, you want it?" She moves her arm near and then far, near and then far.

"You keep it!" Burt gives in. "I don't want to play with you."

51

"Is that what happened? Burt didn't want to play?" Becky does not resist and starts round two of laughter. It's a good moment, bringing up the past to remove the present. Irvin is forgotten, until.....

"Who is that guy, anyway?" Irvin's rare moment of asking Simon anything.

Simon turns toward Irvin, "Why don't you ask him? Isn't this your town?"

"Hey, I talk to who I want to talk to." Irvin puts his hand upon Simon's shoulder and squeezes. "Is that all right with you? Tuck, where's my drink?"

Simon shakes his head and turns away from Irvin. Bob gives a nod of recognition. Simon returns the gesture, then takes a drink of his orange juice, thinking, "Who is this guy?" Bob begins to stroll toward him, jacket draped over his arm, and a glass of water in his hand.

"Yeah, give me a Captain." Irvin tells Tuck, then notices the stranger approaching, "Do you know this guy?" He secretly points. Bob saddles up to the bar, taking the stool next to Simon. "Think they're brothers, Tuck?" Irvin grins as he shuffles his cash, "I'll bet you a million. Ha, ha, ha." Tuck mixes the drink, ignoring the sarcasm, the loneliness, and the hatred.

"You keep your million," as Tuck puts the glass down in front of Irvin.

"What time is it, anyway?" Pat looks for a clock, just being curious.

Burt gets up and looks into the kitchen, the clock facing him from the far wall, "Oh, man, we missed the lottery!"

"The lottery?" Pat questions.

"Yeah, the lottery on channel nine, or is it channel five?"

"You play the lottery?" Pat is in disbelief.

"Yeah, but I never check to see if I win or not." He pulls out his wallet and reaches for a stack of short papers. He picks the papers from his wallet and tosses them at Pat, "See? I've never cashed them in."

"Then why play? Are you goofy or what?" Pat scans the numbers.

"Maybe he's satisfied." Kim covers with an excuse.

Burt sits back down in his chair. "Yeah, I have everything I need!" He holds his arms out wide while his face creates one big smile. Pat scans the living room, the kitchen, and looks back at Burt.

"And what kind of lamp is that?" The room erupts with more laughter.
"Who won the game, Simon?" A question from Bob.
"We did. We won it with the last shot." Simon replies.
"And I see your friend Becky is in town?" An unexpected question.
"Yeah, and how do you know her?" Simon's lost, and confused.
"I've known her for some time, now. Ever since she graduated from high school, actually." Bob takes a drink from his glass and sets it back down. "Well, you have a good night, and watch out for your friends. Okay?"
"Uh, yeah. Whatever." Simon's lost, and confused.
Bob walks by Simon and puts his hand on Irvin's back. Irvin turns abruptly. Bob stares into his eyes, "Having a good night, Magic?"
"Are you really, Burt? You have everything you need?" Pat calms the laughter and gets serious.
"Yeah, I'm satisfied! I have my tunes, my house, my smoke, and my Pay-per-view!" He nods in appreciation, a life worth living.
"And that's all you need?" Pat questions a different man than the one she once knew, or didn't she really know? "How about sex? How about a family?"
"Oh, now I could ask you the last two questions. Where's your sex and family?" Burt counters.
Becky and Kim watch as if it were a tennis match. Pat wants Burt to answer, but Burt keeps digging for Pat's response. They go back and forth, the score remains love-love. Personal issues are hard to score on.
"Hey, who are you?" Irvin's nerves question the man at his side.
"Just relax, I'm an old friend of yours. Here, I'll buy you a drink and then you'll remember. Mr. Jones, may I have a Captain here, please? And make it a double." Bob puts his bills on the bar.
"Hey, thanks! I still can't remember your face, though."
"Okay, Burt, if you're not gonna answer the sex question, how about the money question." Pat tires of the scoreless volleys.
"Money question? What do you mean?"

52

"This!! Why do you play the lottery?" Pat holds up the tickets.

"To make a state donation, aren't I nice?"

"Your nuts, is what you are!" Pat exclaims and throws the tickets at Burt. He laughs, a good old-fashioned belly laugh.

Becky and Kim turn towards Pat in awe. Becky has to speak, "You could be throwing away a million dollars! Don't you think we should cash them in? I mean, what if they're waiting for us?"

"Who's waiting?" Burt pops down the footrest and stands up. "Someone standing outside the window? Becky! Look outside!" He points out the window, behind Becky's head.

"What!" Becky jumps up and away from her chair. "There's no one out there." Burt bends over in laughter. "You shit! Man, I oughtta kick your ass!"

Burt straightens up, turns toward Becky, and places his hand under her chin, "Please."

"You're getting weird." Pat and Kim share her view. She backs away from Burt and notices the tickets in his chair, which fell from his lap when he jumped up. "Should we check these out?" She points to the tickets.

"Take 'em. I don't care." Burt shrugs his shoulders.

"You would throw away a million dollars?" Becky asks, just to make sure.

"I'm sure I already have. Haven't you?" He puts the room in thinking mode, past reflections and future considerations. How much have we spent?

"Um, I don't think so." Becky stays away from the personal issues. She picks up the tickets. "Are we going back to Serby's?"

"You guys go ahead. I've had quite a bit for one day." Burt strolls over to his chair, patting Becky on the shoulder as they trade places. "But, I sure liked having you all over. Thanks!" He nestled in his chair, footrest back up. A comfortable man in a comfortable world.

The ladies grabbed their purses and started the journey back to Serby's, "See you, Burt! We love ya." The front door closes. The snow remains to fall, the wind whispers in the dark corner lot. A street light in the distance leads them back.......

"You'll remember, Magic. Just give it time. In the meantime enjoy your drink." A pat on the back.

"You're not going to give me any more clues? How about a first name?" Irvin pushes for identity.

"Would you give me a million dollars if I told you?" A cold-stare and a stern grin, seriousness.

"Huh? You want a million dollars? Forget it!" A nod of the head and a cold shoulder, Irvin takes a drink from his glass. Bob leans forward, leaving a message in his ear.

"What if I save your life? Isn't that worth a million dollars?" Irvin snaps his head to the right and no one is there. He twists to check out the whole room, and then turns back to his drink. He checks out the glass, stirring the ice cubes with his straw. Tuck steps in front of him. He abruptly looks up.

"Hey, what's wrong with you? Ya look like you seen a ghost."

Isn't that the time everything happens? Cinderella, Cinderella!

At the stroke of midnight all is well, and then, on that full moon, a hallowed night of strange occurrences, mysterious happenings, shadows, and nightmares come to life.

Is it your imagination? Is it your 'fix'? Did not you want to get here? The feeling of fear, the feeling of electricity, "is this how it feels?", and then the paranoia sets in. Are you alone?

"No ghosts." Irvin shook his head. He tried recognizing the image locked in his mind, no remembrance of the character registered. "Just some dude saying I knew him." He takes a sip. "I don't know, maybe my imagination." He replays the last few minutes and knocks on Simon's shoulder, "Hey, did you know that guy?"

Simon turns, "Just a stranger in town. He seems to know everyone, though. I think his name is Bob." He turns back to the television.

"Hey, where did he go?" Irvin wants to link his disappearance to something.

"I don't know. He seems to always disappear," Simon turns and puts a cold-stare into Irvin, "right before your very eyes."

"Hey, Simon," Tuck intervenes, "lay off. I think you're scaring the shit out of this guy."

"Yeah, Simon, quit freaking me out." Irvin's security lay behind the voice of Tuck. He takes a drink from his glass, wiping away the mysterious image.

Brrr, open that door!" Pat shivers as Kim reaches for the handle. The ladies enter Serby's practically unnoticed. They stroll over to Simon and take their seats, one by one. There's a few patrons taking up table space, joking about the weather, telling work-related complaints, work-related affairs, and what is the real differences between the bordered states, Minnesota and Iowa. "Hey, Simon."

"You made it back. How's the weather going?"

"Cold and snowy! Brrr!" Pat removes her jacket, while Kim and Becky decide to leave their's on.

"Can I buy you anything? A Pepsi or Orange Juice?" Simon Serious.

"Yeah, and put some Vodka in it!" Pat completed. Simon thumbed through the cash he had on the bar, pulling out a ten-spot. Tuck stands in waiting for the complete order.

"And what will we be having?" Tuck eyes Kim and Becky.

"I'll have a Slow-Screw, please." Becky, delicious and inviting.

"Make that two." Kim ante's up.

"And you want a Screwdriver?" Tuck asks Pat, just making sure.

"Yes, with Absolut." Like there's really a difference.

"Now, don't be going over the edge!" Irvin peeks his head in between Pat and Simon.

"You still around here?" Pat leans back.

"Can't we just talk? I am sorry for this afternoon."

"And how about an hour ago?"

"Hey, that reminds me, I've got something in the truck!" Simon bolts out of his stool. "The cash is right there for the drinks, Tuck! I'll be right back!" Simon heads out the front door. Everyone stops and wonders what Simon is up to. Irvin cuts into Pat's interest.

"Hey, an hour ago, all we were doing is bullshitting and then we went and cut up some lines. That's it! I swear!"

"I know. Becky told me." Pat agrees, but still remains unsure of her future, and if she lets up on Irvin they'll be back together, and then what. Same old-same old?

"Okay," Irvin puts his drink down on the bar, puts his one hand on Pat's shoulder and tries to convince with the other, "how about a handshake?

Friends for now and what happens, happens. No commitments and no strings, but I will be here for you."

Pat's eyes move around Irvin's face and zero in on his eyes. She takes his hand. "Friends!"

"Thank you. Now, may I sit here?" Tuck sets the drinks down in front of the ladies.

"Well, Simon is sitting there."

54

"That's okay." Irvin puts his hands up, then grabs his drink, and goes back to his stool. "See, I'm still right here." Pat smiles, she feels warm. Becky and Kim taste the beverages and start thumbing through the lottery tickets, which Becky pulled out of her purse. Simon comes busting through the door. "Is he freaking out?" Tuck shrugs his shoulders, he never knew what Simon would be doing next.

Simon darts over to his stool, a small cloth bag in hand, "Here it is! Remember I was telling you about it last night?" He directs to Tuck.

"Sort of, but you never showed it to me."

"Yeah, it was getting late, but here it is!" He starts pulling wooden pieces out of the bag, "Say, do you have any dice?" He suggests to Tuck, while pulling out long pieces, a couple short pieces, and a dozen or so circular pieces. "And here's the directions!" He pulls out a burnt piece of paper.

"What you have, Simon?" Kim had gotten up from her stool and now stood behind him.

"It's my board game, 'Over The Edge'!" Tuck sets down the dice cup used for 'shake-a-day'.

"Hey, I didn't get my shake, today!" Pat grabs for the cup and starts shaking.

Tuck gives Simon the 'ladies first' routine. "Guess ya gotta wait." Pat rolls out five sixes. "Oh, man, I don't believe it!"

"Give me the pot, Tucker-boy!" Five-of-a-kind takes all but five percent. "Here's your dice, Simon!" A small roar of laughter from the bar, except for Simon. He doesn't gamble. Tuck grabs the money jar, twisting off the lid, and reaches in to get the cash. He counts the bills, leaves nine dollars (five percent) and hands the winnings over to Pat. "And drinks for everyone!"

In the meantime, Simon has taken out two dice from the cup and sets up his game. Four steps leading to a platform, which stands on two smaller pieces of wood. "Okay, now you take turns shaking the dice. Irvin, want to play?" Since he crept his way over to Simon's side.

"Sure, I'll try it!"

"Okay, go ahead and roll first, these are your pieces." He sweeps nine of the circular tokens toward Irvin. Irvin rolls a five. "Okay, now, you go up the outside and down the inside. Move five places. Now, it's my turn." Simon rolls a six and moves his piece. "Go ahead, your turn!"

"What's the meaning?" Irvin rolls a two and questions if he can move the same piece or add another to the trail.

"Yep, you can move as many as you want, but the trick is coming down. So, if you want to move this piece," he points at the token on the five space, "count two and you fall in the hole."

"Oh, no. I'm not falling in no hole! I'll move another one." Irvin picks up another token and places it on the board. "Is there any other tricks I should know about?"

"Two more." Simon takes a time-out to explain. "If you land on a step already occupied by the other player you challenge each other for that step. You each shake the dice, low person goes in the hole. And the other way to lose a token is if you land on the trademark and the other player is already on it."

"So, if I land here," Irvin points to the trademark, 'Over The Edge', "and you already have a token on there, I lose my token?"

"No, we both lose our token. We both go in the hole."

"Cool! Let's keep playing. This isn't too bad of a game, for you, any-way." Simon only hears the compliment and shakes the dice, rolling a six.

The game continues, everyone stands around the contestants, it's new, it's exciting, and it's different.

"So, you gonna tell them the real meaning. Like you did me, last night?" Tuck pushes for the real concept, a lesson of truth and understanding, while he sets down four drinks and prepares the next one, an orange juice for Simon. "Pat, you're getting the whole place?"

"Yes the whole place!" She waves her arm as if introducing the next act.

"Okay," Simon rolls a four and moves down from the platform, "it's about running away. See, it's easy to run away, but the hard part is getting back home."

"I see," Pat catches the message, or does she?

"What do you mean, running away?" Becky questions how a game can be an example of reality.

"Have you ever ran?" Kim butts into the topic, putting Becky on the spot. Truth or dare?

"I've ran, but it wasn't up no stairs!"

"Oh, so you're like my other game?" Simon pushes for identity and truth. Tuck comes across the bar with his orange juice. "Thanks for the juice, Pat."

55

"What? You have a game for everybody? Are you some kind of a weirdo or what?" Becky's wall is being knocked into and she's not liking it. Her defenses of name-calling and put-down are coming out, but against Simon they will not work.

"Maybe we should have a private lesson, huh?" Simon stands tall, ready for her comeback. He takes a sip from his glass.

"We had one once, remember?" Becky digs into the two-years-ago serenade. "And what I recall is a boy who couldn't get it up!" She throws the heavy artillery, a man's worst fear-sexual performance.

Simon takes it as if he were wearing a metal vest, "And I had my reasons. Number one is I was drunk."

"Like that has anything to do with it!" Becky Blind.

"Oh yeah it does!" Irvin knows this one. Tuck is ready for some input of his own, but he does have drinks to deliver. Free ones!

"Whatever! So, what was your other reasons, then?" Becky continues. Pat and Kim back up from the turmoil and observe.

Simon looks down at his board game, "How many drugs did we do? The water and trust. There's three more reasons. You need anymore?"

"The water? I thought that was only in Mexico!" Pat steps forward, she has to know.

"Water shrinks things!" Simon cups his privates. The ladies laugh, at an unknown reality?

"You better quit swimming, Simon!" Kim gives him a light punch on the shoulder, still laughing. "Oh, I gotta get away from you. You're silly!"

"But it's true!" Simon smiles, knowing from experience and an episode of 'Seinfeld', he does not stand alone. "It happens."

"Say, we gonna finish this game?" Irvin rather play than to get personal. "It's your turn."

Simon shakes the dice and a five appears. He moves his token onto an occupied space. "Guess it's challenge time." Simon and Irvin shake their dice. Simon rolls a three while Irvin's dice rolls against the wooden step. It falls back showing a two. "And your piece goes into the hole. And being that was your last token all I have to do is make it home." He moves his token home, the board is cleared. "Count your tokens. I have seven."

"I have five, and six." Irvin comes up short. "Shit! You beat me on the last challenge! Want a rematch?" He slams down the remainder of one drink and sets the free drink in its place.

"Maybe someone else." Simon suggests. "How about you, Pat?" He steps back, glass in hand.

"I can do it. We're friends, right?" Pat seems a little timid, but she's pushing herself. Just like all the other times. Irvin takes another drink. She picks up the dice.

"Hey, I go first!" Irvin demands. He rolls a six and the game begins. Pat waits her turn. Kim takes a seat and Becky follows her.

"Isn't he a jerk?" Becky lowers her head to Kim's ear.

Kim turns, "Not my problem. We tried."

Becky sits down, "Need a cigarette?" She pulls the pack out of her purse and takes out two smoking sticks. "You have a light? I seemed to lose mine." As if she even looked.

"I'll take one of those," Pat turns away from the game and points to the cigarette pack. Becky gives her one. "And a light?"

"Here," Simon extends his arm between Becky and Pat, holding a flame.

"Thanks, Simon."

"It's your turn, Patricia!"

"Okay. I'm still going to kick your ass!" She turns back to the game and rolls a two. Simon directs his attention to Becky and Kim. He now stands in between them. Tuck is back behind the bar, looking busy. The music stops to play, but the noise level from the four women at the corner table carries on. The two couples at the near table decide to leave, even though their glasses remain with certain levels of beverage.

"Tuck, aren't you going to play more tunes?" General Irvin Baker.

"Might as well, huh?" Tuck opens the cash register and takes out two dollars. He checks with his bar stool customers, "Everything all right?" No response means everyone is doing fine. He leaves the bar and strolls to the jukebox. He checks out the selections and hits his choice, sort of a Fonzy-punch. No money needed, just the punch.(insert your favorite Elvis song)

56

"Hot-Stuff!" The four women scream. "Is your ass as hard as your hit?" Is there anything better than getting a bartender to blush? How about a bartender who lets you find out your own answers? Tuck inserts the two dollars and plays magnet-from-a-distance. He feels the eyes. The women challenge each other, one stands up, then sits back down, another one stands up and starts taking steps toward Tuck, but turns back around. His choices are selected and he purposefully walks close to their table. A hand reaches out as he walks by and grabs, "It's hard!"

"And do we need anything else?" Tuck teases politely. Giggles fill the air.

In the meantime Becky and Kim are discussing the difference between friendship and romance, Pat and Irvin. Kim believes friendship is just as important while Becky questions the need for commitment. Simon stands in between them, letting their discussion play-out. He does not interfere, only listens.

"And if Pat wants to be pushed by him, let her." Kim is not going to play big-sister, she already sees herself as a mother figure for Becky.

"You don't sound like yourself. I mean, how many times have you told me to drop someone?" Becky counters, expecting Kim to break up the match next to them.

"Maybe I've had enough. Maybe I rather not get involved with other's affairs."

"Oh, but you will mine?"

Kim sticks out her hand, "Not no more. I promise."

Becky pauses, thinking of going it alone, no more security blanket. She straightens up on her stool and takes Kim's hand, "Okay, be that way." They shake hands in silence. Simon strolls over to the window, checking out the weather. Becky and Kim finish their drinks. "Do you need another?"

"Are you buying?" Kim's aware of Becky's gentle persuasion, order first and then stick the other person with the bill.

"Okay. I'll buy this one." Becky reaches into her purse and starts looking for the cash.

"And I move three spaces, one, two, and home. All my tokens are in, how many do you have?" Pat starts to count her tokens while Irvin rolls his dice to see if he can make it home. He rolls a two, straight into the hole.

"Shoot! I didn't make it."

"How many you have? I have six." Pat checks out his tokens.

"Seven. I win!"

"You cheat! I seen you pull that one into your pile. You only have six!"

"Hey! What you doing watching my tokens?"

"Forget it! I'm not playing with you no more. Tuck, may I have a drink, please?"

"Sure thing! And you two ladies?" He points at Becky and Kim.

"Yes, the same." Kim replies. Tuck grabs the bottles and begins to pour, cutting back a little on the alcohol. As if they'll notice. Simon comes walking back to the bar.

"Have you done any shoveling? It's piling up out there." He asks Tuck.

"Shoot no! How bad is it?"

"I'll do it for ya. The shovel in the same place?" Back hallway, leaning against the wall.

"Should be. Thanks!" Tuck sets up the women. "Irvin, how you doing?"

"Just give me a few, but I will buy a pack of smokes. Red box, top shelf." A few drinks and the craving of a cigarette, or does the cigarette hide the taste of the alcohol? Tuck flips him a pack.

"Need matches?" A customary after-thought.

"Yeah, I can always use matches." Irvin reaches into his pocket and pulls out a lighter. Tuck pauses and then tosses him the book of matches anyway. "Thanks." The four women at the corner table start putting on their jackets, still whispering about the bartender. Simon heads out the front door with the shovel.

"Everyone's leaving." Pat notices the empty spaces.

"Well, it's getting that time," Tuck nods toward the bar clock, a commercial in itself with the big hand fifteen minutes fast telling the customers to go home, it's getting late.

"Ah! And you're not staying open late, tonight?" Pat knew how the last few nights had been, especially last night.

"Nope. The boss is breathing down my throat on that one."

"Serby? Hell, he'll let you stay open 'til morning." Irvin helped himself, not the guy behind the bar.

57

Tuck turned his back on the remark and walked over to the table. "See you ladies, again!"

"In our dreams," smiles all around, "but we do have to go home to our husbands." The smiles do a flat-line as the eyes speak of 'hold me'.

"Yeah, and the weather is getting pretty bad." No time to look into eyes. It's too close to closing time, and besides, no married woman for this guy. It was an old memory Tuck would never forget, a friend of a friend getting blown away by a jealous husband. "You ladies take care." He began to pick up the bottles, glasses, and erase the images. And the tips!

The ladies walked on, with Irvin getting a last look. To himself, there was only one who would measure up, but he rather not waste his energy on a gamble. She would look different come morning. "See you, all!" Just in case, they'll recognize me next time.

"What a hound!" Pat notices the flirting, and the arrogance. "I don't know if I even want to be your friend."

"Yeah, and before these two got here you were all over me!" Irvin eyes Kim and Becky.

"Yeah, well, maybe I needed them to point some things out!"

"Like what? How they can destroy a relationship?" Tempers and voices rise.

"No! Like showing me what an asshole you really are!" Kim and Becky stand up and get in between the two conflicts. "I mean, how long have you been pulling shit like this?" referring to the parting wave and wink.

"Hey, I am a guy!" Irvin's excuse, the reason of a true rat.

"Oh, like us girls go around whoring while our boyfriends stay at home?" Becky counters.

"Do you?" Irvin stands unready for a shot between the eyes. Pat grabs her purse. "Where you going?" Irvin grabs her arm.

"Let go, asshole! I'm going where you're not!" She pulls herself away from Irvin, "Come on, girls! We're leaving!"

Becky and Kim take a look at each other, "Um, I guess." Becky replies. "See what you cause?" She directs her statement to Irvin. Pat bolts to the door, while Kim and Becky grab their purses. Becky takes one last drink and looks for Tuck. She spots him still by the table. "Tuck!" He turns. "I'll see you later!"

"Um, okay." He waves, but thinks it might be another girl getting away. Irvin stands as a statue, silent and plastered. The girls file out leaving the place silent. Once again, the bartender is left wondering what happened, but he's used to it. He finishes cleaning the table and walks back in position, behind the walnut, a side judge at this circus waiting for the next act to enter, stage right. The front door opens to the appearance of an over-stuffed jacket, earflaps on an orange hunting cap, and buckle overshoes, it's Simon.

Tuck laughs out loud, "What the hell, boy!"

"It's snowing out there!" Simon's head held high. Even Irvin starts to laugh. Isn't funny how Tuck's last selection, the one starting to play, is 'Grandma Got Run Over By A Reindeer'. "Say, where are the girls going?"

"Didn't you ask?" Irvin couldn't come up with a nickname. Simon heard the question and turned back out the door. "That little shit!"

"Hey, if he wants something he goes after it." Tuck liked his courage.

"Whatever. Give me another drink."

The ladies were one block down and on their way back to Pat's. "What are we going to do, now?" Becky always needed to know the next step.

"Well, it looks like we're going in the direction of Pat's place. Now doesn't it?" Kim always playing mom and big sister. She is tired of it!

"Unless you two know of some other place to go?" Pat adding a bit of sarcasm. They all stopped and stared at each other, eyes wincing and frowns formed. "How about Burt's?"

"Yeah, right! He's crashed I'm sure." Becky does her valley-girl impression.

"Hey, he does have papers." Pat throws it another try. Becky shrugs her shoulders. Kim tilts her head back and looks into the snowflakes. "Kim! Are you with us?"

"Let's start walking." They do an about-face and walk back towards Serby's, but they are not going back in. "Should we stop by and pick up the car?"

58

"No. It's a perfect night for walking." Pat loves the snow, the breeze, the chill. It helps to make her mind numb, forgetting about the past. Forgetting about Irvin and her mom. Just being among nature, a soul without it's personality. They continue to walk in silence, even Becky.

"Well, Irvin, you cleared the place out once again." Tuck tossed the blame to a repeat offender.

"Ah, you were working too hard, anyway. Why don't you make yourself a drink?"

"I don't think so. The last thing I need is to get caught with my fingers in the cookie jar." Tuck emphasizing on the caught.

"I won't say nothing. Who's gonna know?"

"I'll know!" Tuck knew his conscious, he could not tell a lie.

"You sure you want to leave the car? It's cold out here." Becky asked as they approached Serby's parking lot. The temperature hovered around thirty degrees, but the slight breeze and the earlier warm temperatures made it seem colder.

"Keep walking!" Pat answered. "If we take the car, Irvin'll track us down. Copious!"

"Yeah, whatever." Becky lowered her head and kept walking, against the wind. Kim remained silent. They cleared Serby's block, two more to go, when all of a sudden, from their right side, out of the shadows pounced an overstuffed jacket with an orange top. "Ahhh!" It grabbed Becky.

"Ahhhh!" Pat and Kim joined the scream. Pat stepped back, braced herself and started swinging her purse. Kim trotted across the street, they were all wearing high-heels. Becky covered her face and prayed. "You son-of-a-bitch!" Pat kept swinging until the stranger went down. "Leave us alone!" Becky heard a thump and parted her hands. The stranger lay on the ground. Pat stood to the side of him and demanded his appearance. "Show your face!" Kim stood across the street, waiting and ready. The stranger started to get up. "I didn't say to get up, just show your face!" Pat gave her purse a swing. Kim jumped. Becky added a kick to the legs. The hood is parted and the cap removed. "Simon! You asshole!" The purse comes down and the kicking repeats. Kim laughs from the sideline.

"You closing early?" Irvin noticed the late-night ritual performed by the bartender. He had closed many bars, hanging until last-call was like receiving a longevity medal, something he didn't accomplish in the military.

"Yeah. The weather's getting pretty bad and it is getting close, anyway." Tuck wasn't sure on his predictions. Maybe there would be more customers, maybe not. To ask Irvin what he would do would be a mistake and to ponder the thought of what his boss might do, he didn't want to. The day had been long enough. "Yep, last-call!"

"I'll take two!"

After a bit of convincing, actually quite a bit, the ladies let Simon tag along. "But no more jumping out at us!" They bucked the wind and stayed on the street. The town is pretty well deserted and the snow is quite deep on the sidewalks. "Simon, where did you get that outfit?"

"Out of my truck. I'm always prepared for the worst." His hood lay back as he carried his cap in his hand. His head held high feeling the fresh air and the falling of flakes. To him, the wind is an added bonus.

"You're silly!" Kim smiled and took on the same actions as Simon. Why not feel it instead of buck it? The wind and cold are somewhat refreshing, if you let it. Becky remained stomping through the snow, watching each step. Pat checked out the scenery, never focusing on just one thing. Would she ever see it like this, again?

Tuck poured a little extra in Irvin's last drink and set the two glasses in front of him, "There you are, King of Last-call!" Word had gotten out.

"And here's to you! Bottom's up!" Down to the last drop. "Whew. Good stuff."

"One more and we're out of here!" Tuck loved closing time, now it's his turn. These days there is no drinking, but there is always a little smoke to enjoy. "Got any papers?"

"Uh, I don't know." Irvin coughs on an ice cube. "Let me check out my uncle's desk." He sets his glass down and walks to the office. Tuck remains at the bar, turning off the lights, all but one, closing the register, and doing a last-minute tidying. Irvin sits down behind the desk and opens the top right drawer, he's been here before.

"What you looking for?" Mike Serby stands at the doorway of his office.

"Oh, Uncle Serb, just looking." Irvin closes the drawer.

"Well, I told you before to stay out of my personals. Have you been listening?"

"Yeah, I been listening." Irvin stands up.

59

"Then get out! I don't want to see you in this office, again. Understand?" Serby knew Irvin was stuck in a bad place, no parents and an only child, and he tried his best to be big brother and dad. His wife, Martha, tried to be mom. It wasn't easy, especially when his own kids despised him.

"Okay, I understand." Irvin walked from behind the desk and into the hallway, Serby gives him a pat on the back. "Did Martha come down with ya?" Irvin had been trying to keep his guardians together. Word had it, Uncle Mike had been involved in an affair, and Irvin did his best to detour the noise.

"No. Sorry, Irvin, but things aren't looking too good," spoken in a crackling voice. "She decided to stay with her sister. It was a hell of a ride home."

"Anything I can do?" Irvin loved his uncle and aunt. To keep them together would keep himself together, so he thought.

"You've done enough. Believe me, I know you have tried to help and I thank you." Serby's emotions were sad, his facial expression seemed to be holding back tears. "But the best you could do is just to stay out of it. I know you mean well, but this is something me and your aunt have to work out. Now go home before the blizzard keeps you away from your cows."

"Screw the cows, man! I want to stay with you!" Irvin pleads.

"I won't allow it. You owe it to your animals and to your dad. Now, go take care of them." Serby turned away and walked into the bar area, "Hey, Tuck, closing down for the night?" Irvin followed and sat down at his stool, finishing his last drink. Mike had stopped at the end of the bar but after noticing Irvin take a seat he decided to join him. "Say, Tuck, mix us each one more. And include yourself."

"No, thanks. I'm court-ordered and I'm not messing that up." Tuck grabbed the bottle of 'Captain' and poured two drinks.

"I understand. Mix yourself a soda, then, and sit down with us." Mike knew the law and wasn't one to push alcohol, but Irvin sat with a good buzz.

"We're here. Who's going to knock on the door?" the ladies and Simon stood at the end of Burt's sidewalk, at least the snowplows had taken care of the streets.

"I'll do it, since I've got the footwear for it." Simon lifts up his foot showing off his buckles.

"Just go, already! I'm getting cold standing here!" Becky might be wearing a jacket, but she also sports a skirt and high-heels. Kim and Pat are feeling comfortably numb. Simon walks through the half-knee deep snow and knocks on the door, three knocks and a finger roll. No answer. He pounds on the door four times and hears a noise. "Is he in there?"

"I hear something!" The door opens.

"Hey, Simon, what's up?"

"Just a nightcap. Mind if we come in?"

"No. Come on in. Man, it's really been snowing, huh?" The ladies trudge through the snow, Simon holding the door open for them. "Yeah, I fell asleep. What time is it?"

"I don't know," Simon answers. Pat's the first one in and sits at the couch. Kim follows and Becky takes the chair next to the door. Simon closes the door and stands. "You smell something?"

"Yeah, what is that? You got something burning?" Pat inhales the smell of smoke.

"Oh, yeah, my pizza!" Burt rushes into the kitchen and opens up the oven. "Shit! There goes my supper." He throws the toasted disc on top of the oven and shakes his head. "Man, I do this all the time."

"And you were telling us you didn't need a woman?" Pat remembers the earlier conversation.

Burt shrugs his shoulders and sits down in his big chair. "So, you want to smoke one?"

"That's why we're here." Kim answers in a passive manner and turns toward Pat.

"To smoke my dope?" Burt's used to it.

"No! We need papers." Pat clarifies the misunderstanding. Burt reaches under his chair, pulls out a tray, and tosses Pat a book of papers. "And are you going to give me the tray so I can roll it?" Burt looks at the tray and shoves it back under the chair.

"Nah, I'll get you a plate." He gets up and saunters into the kitchen, retrieves a plate, and hands it over to Pat. He then takes a seat and reaches for the stereo, ejecting one tape and picking out another. "How about Dylan?" He holds up the cassette.

60

"We'll take Bob!" Kim shows enthusiasm, having been to a celebrity party with Bob Dylan making a cameo. "I seen him once, and he gave me a kiss right here!" She points to a spot on her right cheek.

"Yeah, we've heard it." Becky can tell you the luxury of living with an ex-model, hearing the stories, but never getting to see the characters. "Do you have any other kind of music."

"Too bad, this one's in!" Burt's place, Burt's rules.

The three remains, Tuck, Irvin, and Serby, had all took a chair around the center table. Being a long and narrow establishment it seemed all the tables were against the wall, and they were. The center table just happened to be behind their bar stools. "So, how was the night?" Serby checking up on his clientele.

"Not bad. A few here and there. One wedding party and the rest just going through."

"Wedding party, huh?" For some reason Tuck sensed a nerve being stung.

"Yeah, and then your usual, Burt and Pat."

"And Pat's friends, Kim and Becky!" Irvin completed the roster.

"Oh, yeah? Where they from?" Serby let the kid talk.

"St. Paul or Minneapolis. Somewhere over there!"

"Minneapolis, hmph." Serby lowered his head. Tuck sensed some bad things going on.

"What's wrong, Serby? Something we said." Tuck dug for some information, trouble-shooting for symptoms. Serby nodded his head and then lifted it, with watery eyes.

"Irvin, I didn't want you to hear this, but your aunt wants a divorce."

"No way! Why would she want that?" Irvin never seen it coming, neither did Serby, but he should have. When you're sleeping around, what do you expect?

"We have to work this out. That's why I told you to be quiet and go home."

"Oh, just go take care of the cows! That's all I'm good for?" Irvin slammed the remainder of his drink and then slammed it down on the table. "I don't get you!" He then got up from his chair and bolted to the door. Tuck got up and began to follow, until Serby stopped him.

"Just let him go! He'll feel better about the whole thing, tomorrow." Serby looked down at his glass, making small circles with it. Tuck sat back down across from him. Irvin stomped and kicked his way to the truck, swearing and cussing.

"What the heck has he been doing? I wonder if he did screw around on Aunt Martha. Coke-head!" He came up to his truck and noticed something very peculiar, it had snowed all over except for on his truck. His truck had barely any snow on it. "Who did this?" He seen the Grand-Am, same thing, hardly any snow on it. "Probably Simon, that little son-of-a-bitch, always doing favors." Irvin jumped in the truck, started it, cranked on the tunes, and barreled out. "Maybe I can make last-call at Siskatown."

A gathering place, small and serene, not much action and always inviting. A few hungry souls, their menu consisting of interaction, adventure, and a comfort zone. Just to get away!

Getting away from family, an argument (win or lose), stubbornness, and blinding ears. Too much to handle at the office. A co-worker who took your job. The neighbor who cut into your lawn, going over the invisible borderline.

Do your problems disappear at the local watering hole? Where do they go and who did you give them to? Is your family going to listen now that you've had a couple? Maybe your boss will walk in and offer you the job back—as if you would take it!

Closing time is over and the door opens for your exit—ready for reality?

Irvin passed by Burt's place, noticed the light on and grumbled, "Yeah, you all have fun! I can manage on my own. Siskatwon has better women anyway!" He's off to the races, five miles west on Highway 122, against the wind and the snow. His digital clock reads ten minutes before last-call.

"Tuck?" Serby needed information on a bad situation, "How did you handle your divorce?" He looked up from the table, sheepishly. Tuck sat across from him, expecting the worst.

"Time. Lots of time and self-reflection."

"Huh? What's self-reflection?" His mind is interested, but his comprehension is weak.

"When you look in the mirror, what do you see?" Tuck starts the examination.

"I don't look in no mirror!" Serby takes the last drink from his glass and pushes the glass toward Tuck, "Fill this up!"

"Please?"

"I pay you, I don't have to say please. Now, fill it up!"

Tuck gets up from his chair, grabs the glass, and walks over to the bar. "I'll fix him one, all right." He pours the glass half full of alcohol and fills the rest of it with soda. Serby's finger-drawing on the table. Tuck struts back to the table and sets down the glass, "Here you go, boss!"

"Thanks. You're a good man, Tuck." Tuck takes his seat and sips a little bit of his soda, checking Serby's reaction to his first swallow—there is none. "Now, about this mirror thing. I do have one in my office. You want to check it out?"

"And to think Zimmerman is from good old Minnesota! The first guy to put our country's politics on the defense. I think that's cool!" Burt never voted because he believed in each person being accountable for themselves. It's the government wanting to get involved in the individual, not the other way around.

"Yep, pretty cool!" Pat second the motion. "Is there anything left of that joint?"

Becky had put the roach on the edge of the ashtray, "Just a little." She lifted it up, showing it to Pat. "You want it?"

"Nah. Burt do you have anything to drink?"

"Not here, my fridge is always empty. If I want a beer I go to Serby's. Sort of makes me get out of the house, you know what I mean?" Living on his own there is always a risk of boredom and depression, cabin-fever in the north country.

"Yeah! I know what you mean." Kim answered. "When I was pregnant and couldn't get anywhere, depressing, and frustrating. Especially when everyone else I knew would be going to Premieres and Modeling Galas. That was the longest nine months of my life."

"And then to lose it." Becky finished the tribulation. The room becomes silent, Bob starts up on 'A Rolling Stone', the wind howls in the background, and eyes begin to shut, all taking their separate vision. Even Becky stops looking around and enjoys her inner peace.

Snow drifts cross the path of a wildman, he laughs at each hit, sneers at the blizzard as if in competition with the gods, "Bring it on, Snowman!" Two miles from his destination, the clock reads five more minutes. His hands clutch the steering wheel tightly, his eyes focused on each approaching drift, every once in awhile veering off to the clock, "I'm gonna make it, I'm gonna make it."

Tuck followed Serby's lead, right into the back office. Serby takes a seat behind the desk, opening the left top drawer, and pulls out a mirror. "Now, how does this self-reflecting thing work?" Tuck picks up the folding chair against the wall and moves it in front of the desk. He sits down as Serby picks up a straw from inside the drawer, "Is this how you do it?"

62

"Uh, not what I was thinking, but if you want to." Tuck let Serby play out his emotions and actions not wanting to cause a disagreement, besides Cocaine used to be his favorite. Serby flipped through some notepads in the drawer and found his 'butterfly'. He placed it on the desk. "You want to do the chopping?"

"No blades!" Tuck has second-thoughts, his ex-wife, the drug dealers who sold him out. Maybe Serby would have to forfeit this one, no cutting tools—no cocaine.

"I always have blades! You think I'm stupid?" Tuck remains silent as the mirror is pushed toward him, along with the necessary tools. "Make 'em fat!"

Drift after drift the course becomes habitual, the clock reads three more minutes. The town lays directly ahead, with the bar located on the east side, right on the edge of town. Irvin's focused, he's going to make it, clock, drift, clock, drift, a blur—'Whump'! The steering wheel jolted to the right, he hung onto it and pushed it back around to the left. The truck veered one way and then another. He applied the brakes and cut back to the right and the truck spun halfway around, his lights now shining in the direction he came from, but at least he came to a stop. "Whew! Holy cats!" His limbs are trembling as he looks around for other vehicles, no one to be seen. He pushes down on the accelerator, the tires only spin. He tries reverse, but the tires only spin.

Tuck straightens out two lines and pushes the mirror to Serby, "You're the host!"

"Thanks, Tuck." Serby accepts the mirror and picks up the straw. He lifts his arms as if performing the last note for the orchestra, he shakes his hands and takes a deep breath. His hands stop, he holds his breath, and then releases. "Time for action!" He bends his head down, places the straw close to his nose, and follows the white line, inhaling lightly.

"Damn, six inches from being unstuck!" Irvin had gotten out of the truck and checked the situation, a dead deer and his back tire stuck in a snow drift. Luckily he carried a shovel. He reached for the shovel and put it to work.

"Good stuff, Tuck! Here you go," he slid the mirror to Tuck and set the straw down in front of him. Serby continued to take deep inhales and then reached for a little extra, "I forgot the numb."

"Uh, I don't know, Serb. Maybe I shouldn't be doing this." Tuck has second thoughts and a conscience, if he says it's bad for one person to do then how can he do it. His ex-wife is very much on his mind. "The court system and all..."

"Screw them! How they gonna know about this? Cocaine leaves your system in a very short time, take it!" Serby pushes the mirror a little closer to Tuck and stares into his eyes. Tuck breaks and sets the straw under his nose. He begins to follow the white line. "There you go!" Serby takes a drink from his glass.

Irvin throws the shovel to the side and hops into the truck. He shifts it into drive, pushes lightly on the accelerator. "Almost!" He shifts into reverse and then back into drive. He continues the process about seven times, and he brakes free. "All right!" He opens the door, jumps out, throws the shovel in the box, and looks at the deer. "Too bad, I've got better things to do!" He jumps back into the truck and turns it back toward Siskatown. "They know me, I'll still get last-call."

"Ah, am I high," Pat opened her eyes, as if you could tell. "Do you have any cards or anything?"

"How about something to eat?" Becky has the craving for chocolate, chips, peanuts, pretzels, candy...

"Or something to drink? Even a soda?" Kim experiences dry-mouth, cotton-mouth, and a fuzzy mind.

Burt reaches on top of his stereo and pulls down a board, "Here, how about some Cribbage?"

"And did you hear us?" Becky scolds.

"Yeah, just wait. I think I have a big bottle of soda." He gets up from his chair, waddles into the kitchen, opens the fridge, and pulls out a big bottle. He shuts the door and carries the bottle into the living room, "We can share."

"So, Tuck, self-reflection work for you?" Serby had gotten up from his chair, putting his hands down on his desk. He looked directly into Tuck's eyes when asking.

"Sometime." Tuck felt the early effects and knew what to expect. He tried to stay in control.

"Well, I tell you what," Serby came around the desk and placed his hand on Tuck's shoulder. "I have my own little remedy for lost causes. Let's go back in the bar, I have something to show you."

63

Burt had found a box in his hall closet and made it into a makeshift table, setting it down in front of the couch. He placed the Cribbage board on it and Pat began to shuffle the cards, "So, who's partners?"

"Wait a minute," Kim looked around the room, "where's Simon?"

Burt moved his chair up to the table, "I don't know. He must've left." He sat down and removed the game pieces from beneath the board.

Becky turned around in her chair and lifted the curtain, "There he is! He's shoveling snow!" She laughed and adored the scene.

Kim walked over to the window, "He's so silly!" Pat also got up and came to the window. She smiled, and felt secure, warm on the inside. Burt picked up the cards and started to shuffle. He then dealt out the cards for four players.

"Made it! Time for a good drink." Irvin pulled in front of the East-Side Tavern, shut off the engine, checked out his hair, and opened the door. The snow lightened up and the wind calmed. He jumped out of the truck and strutted to the front door.

Serby approached the bar and directed Tuck to go behind the Walnut, "See that little wooden box? Right there in the corner." Serby knew exactly where it sat.

"Yeah." Tuck seen it, but didn't know if he should lift it, or touch it.

"Well, bring it up here!" Serby patted the bartop. Tuck lifts it out of the corner and places it in front of Mike Serby. "It's the best thing I have! Open it up." Serby levels his eyes into Tuck's and pushes the box toward him. Tuck adheres to the order and opens it.

"You guys playing, or not?" Burt questions, then reaches for another cassette (insert Heavy Metal). The ladies giggle as they watch the guy with the shovel. It's as if he's putting on a show, dancing with each stroke and scoop, but the sidewalk is only so long.

Irvin opens the door, takes a deep breath, and walks in. No cover charge. He strolls to the nearest stool and checks out his surroundings. No bartender behind the bar. "Shoot, I must've missed it," he whispers. He pulls out his cash, if nothing else he'll buy some peanuts. Someone grabs his hand.

"I remember you!" A sweet, tender voice. Automatically inviting.

"Ah, do you?" Irvin tries to focus on the facial outline. She smiles broadly. "Oh, yeah, at Serby's. Just awhile ago!"

"Yes, you waved at me," totally inviting. "And then you gave me a wink?"

"Uh, yeah, I did." Irvin looks around for any sightseers. Where's the bartender?

"I'm not with anyone, if you're wondering. And you missed last-call."

"Oh, guess I'm out of luck, then."

"Like I said, I'm not with anyone. Do you want to take me home?"

Simon shoved the shovel into a snowbank and walked back to Burt's door, he knocked. Kim, standing right next to the door, having watched his every step, opened it. "You're so silly, Simon!"

"Someone has to be. Mind if I come in?" Kim backed up and allowed him to enter, whereupon he removes his coat and buckle overshoes. Burt remains silent as Becky and Pat are caught in a trance, just watching this pleasant, comforting image make himself at home. "You all didn't see Irvin about thirteen minutes ago, did you?" The trance is snapped.

"No!" Pat exclaims. "Where you see him?" Becky holds her back, gently with one hand on Pat's shoulder. Kim remains watching Simon, hearing but not listening. Burt stands up and turns down the stereo.

"He left town, going toward Siskatown."

"Huh? Why would he go there?" Pat needed explanation, but no one could give it.

"I don't know," Simon admitted.

"Maybe, he knows someone?" Burt implied.

"Pat, weren't you going to stay away from him?" Becky with a comforting anecdote.

"You're right. I have to let go," Pat listened not only to her friend, but also to herself. "Should we play cards?"

"You like what you see?" Mike Serby takes pride in his wares, especially this one. "Bought it brand new just a couple of weeks ago. She's the best thing I have. She's my sweetheart!" Tuck remained looking in the box, transfixed on it's contents—an Ivory handled revolver, a piece you would find in a George S. Patton photograph. "Take her out of the box!" Serby instructed.

64

"Uh, I don't...." Tuck didn't want to touch it, really.

"Come on!" Serby turned the box around and grabbed the revolver. "It's just a gun!" Lifting it into the air, admiring the shine, the barrel, and the handle. "But this one's a beauty," almost a whisper.

"What you going to do with it?"

"Huh? What do you mean, what am I going to do with it?"

"I don't know," Tuck shrugs his shoulders.

"I like nice things and this is a nice thing. I'm gonna keep it! That's what I'm gonna do with it."

"Oh, that's cool."

"And maybe shoot me some pigeons if that's all right with you." Serby levels his eyes into Tuck's.

"Uh, yeah, shoot as many as you want. I don't care," Tuck backs up from the bar, wanting to get out of the trap he feels he's in.

"You don't care? Now, Tuck, we all must care." Serby holds the revolver in one hand and reaches for the box of shells with the other.

Tuck's nerves are beginning to show, he feels hot, tense, "Say, how long we staying open?"

"Huh? Didn't you lock the doors?" A brief interruption from Serby opening the small box.

Irvin looked down at his hands, then up to the clock, and then back into her eyes, "What did you say?"

"Do you want to take me home?" She waits patiently for his answer, soft and surreal.

"Um, I could, I guess." Hands sweaty, mind stuck on unbelievable.

"Should we go then?" She sets her drink down and gazes back into his eyes.

"Uh, yeah, okay," he gets up from the stool, puts his arm around her, and they begin to walk. "Wait a minute," he sees her glass on the bar, half full, "I might need this." He then empties the glass.

Burt and Pat sat across from each other as partners, playing against Kim and Becky. "Okay, partner, we have to start out good."

"You deal me some good cards and it'll be no problem." Simon knelt down close to the make-shift table and observed. The volume had been appropriately readjusted to accommodate the mood, right around channel seven. "Is there any soda left in that bottle?"

"Uh, let me check," Tuck moved from behind the bar.

"Hey! Don't you want to join me in some target practice?" Tuck froze. Serby starts loading the revolver, "Come on, we'll use the dart board!" A grin across his face.

"Hey, Simon should be coming to get me soon! How about you just practice with yourself?" Wrong answer from another person.

"What? You been talkin' to my old lady? That's exactly what she said!" The revolver loaded, he points it at the dart board, and fires! "Bullseye!!"

"Fifteen for two," Burt moves his peg ahead two spaces. "Was Tuck coming over after he closes up? He's a pretty nice guy."

"I don't know. We all just left. Do you know, Simon?"

"What time is it? Maybe I'll just go back over there, and get my truck."

"Okay. Could you bring back something to drink?" Pat holds up the empty soda bottle.

"That'll be up to him," Simon stands up and puts his coat on. "Lay down this card," he points to the Jack of Hearts in Becky's hand.

"What if I don't want to?"

"Then don't. Just trying to help out." She lays down the Jack, "Thirty one for two and a go. See you all in a bit." He opens the door and vanishes into the wind and snow.

"He's so cool," Kim swoons. Becky sneers. Burt starts out with the five of clubs.

Irvin opens the door and softly guides her with his hand, a calm night after all. Are dreams really true? Do they happen before or after you go to sleep? They stroll to his truck and he opens the passenger door, the dome light comes on.

A shot rings out, Tuck's nerves bounce. He glances at Serby, a grin on his face and laughter in his voice, "Did I make you jump? Should I do it, again?"

"Hey!" Tuck yells, out of fear. "Aren't you gonna let me try?" He has no idea where the words come from or why his feet start to move toward the wildman with the Ivory handle, his hands open.

65

"Ah, I don't know. You didn't want to before, and now you do?" He holds the revolver, in a suspicious state of mind. "You're not going to run away with it, are you?"

"No, Serb. I want to try it out," he keeps walking closer, but slowly. Serby points the gun at the dartboard and fires! Tuck stops, remains silent.

"You know, I did have another gun, something like this one, but it's missing. You didn't take it, did you?" He points the gun at Tuck. "I don't like people stealing things."

Tuck rises his arms, "I stand innocent, man. I don't like stealing, neither."

"What, uh, where?" Irvin wakes up, being knocked out when he hit the deer. His truck swerved completely around. He's lucky it didn't roll over.

"You all right, son?"

"Huh? Dad is that you?" He looked into a flashlight, then noticed the flashing in his rearview mirror, blue, red, and white. "Shit....."

"Mr. Baker, will you turn the engine off, please," commanded the highway patrol. Irvin turned the key and wiped his face with his right hand. "Can you get out your door?" Another officer stood outside the driver's door.

"I tell you what, Tuck. Why don't you just go home? I need a little space."

"Um, okay. You sure I can't get anything for you before I leave?"

"Nah," he checks out the engraving on the revolver. "Ya know this is a replica." He holds the gun steady in his palm.

"That's cool, Serb. I'll see you on Monday, then?"

"Yeah, we'll see ya. You have a good night." Tuck escaped out the back door and ran down the alley. He knew Burt was Serby's best friend and he ought to know his condition—unstable!

"Mr. Baker. Have we been meeting just a little too often?" The officer questioned upon Irvin's exiting from his truck. "Have you been drinking tonight?"

"A little. I was at my uncle's place," Irvin confirmed his whereabouts.

"And you're facing west?" The snow and the wind had covered his tracks, but the officers were wondering how he had hit the deer and ended up where he was. "Now, where else were you?" The officer questioned deeper, checking for slur of speech and memory loss.

"Just there," Irvin remembered the girl, but couldn't place where she was. He looked around, confused.

"Well, we're giving you a breath test," the officer held a small device and held it up to Irvin's mouth, "Blow into the tube, please." Irvin blew until one of the lights shown up. In his case, the wrong one. "You remember hitting that deer?" he flashed a light on the dead corpse.

"Oh, wow." Irvin put his hand to his forehead. He knew the place he was in was not a good one.

Tuck ran down the alley and hooked a left, running toward Main Street. He then turned a right, noticing a figure walking towards him. "Hey! Who are you?"

"Simon! Is that you, Tuck?"

"Yeah," Tuck stopped, but continued to yell, "get Burt! Serby's going crazy, man! Go get him!" Simon turned and ran back to Burt's, while Tuck trotted back to Serby's. "Man, just don't kill yourself."

"Which squad car we putting him in? Did you call for a tow truck?" one officer talking to another.

"Tow truck should be here shortly, but the weather could cause delays." Mr. Highway Patrol confirmed. "I'll stay here and wait. You go ahead and transport him to Hontra. Leave your radio off so no one bothers you. You might have to check him out for a concussion, too."

"I hear ya." The officer took Irvin by the arm and escorted him to the backseat.

Simon hit the door, running, "Burt!"

"What the hell, boy! Scare the shit out of all of us!" Burt practically tipped over in his chair. All the girls jumped, especially Pat, who was ready to lay down the winning card.

"Hey, Serby's going crazy!" Simon didn't notice the reactions, he was there to save a life. "We gotta go down there! Come on, let's go!" Simon turned right back out the door, waited a mille-second and began to run.

"What was that all about?" Becky demanded.

66

"I don't know, but I'm not waiting to find out!" Burt got out of his chair, grabbed his coat from the kitchen chair, and started to bolt. "Come on! Don't just sit there!" Pat looked at Kim, then at Becky. "Come on, Pat, we gotta go!"

Tuck came up the back steps, slowly. He didn't want to alarm Serby, but he did want to ease his situation. "This sucks, man." He reached for the handle and pulled, "he locked it. Man, hang on." Tuck's hands trembled, his heart raced, and he took a deep breath, "just chill. I'll just have to go to the front." He went down the steps and began to run.

The patrol officer radioed in his whereabouts and suspect description, "I have a possible concussion, DWI, and hit-and-run. I'm bringing him in!"

"Ten-four. How's the weather?"

"Not good, and it's getting worse. Luckily the snowplow noticed this guy." No return comment and the officer shut the radio off. "Peace and quiet, it's gonna be a long ride." Irvin sat silent, confused, and dazed—what exactly happened?

Tuck came around to the front of Serby's just as Simon showed up, "The other's are coming! You think we should wait?"

"Yeah, we'll wait," Tuck didn't want to bust in on this one. "Burt can talk to him, hopefully."

"She wants a divorce? Poor little Martha, as if I haven't given her everything she ever needed, including a swift kick-in-the-ass every once in awhile! Ha, ha, ha!" Serby danced around, swinging his revolver in the air. "Stupid bitch should have known better than to ever saddle up with me! And now where is she? Where's her kids?" He paused for a moment and glanced at the gun. "Yeah, where's my kids?" spoken softly he hit his own nerves. The room became quiet, still, and empty.

"Here they come," Simon spoke lightly upon noticing Burt approaching. The ladies are about half a block away. "You have the key, right?"

"Yeah, I forgot all about it." Tuck reached into his pocket and pulled out four keys on a ring. "It's this one right here." Burt approached, slightly winded.

"Is he still in there?" Burt asked.

"Yeah, we seen him through the window. He's swinging a gun around!"

"Oh, shit. Well, are we going in?" Burt stood ready, better now than too late. Tuck stuck the key into the door and turned, unlocking it. "You want me to go in first?"

"Yeah," Tuck's hands still shake. "Are you ready?"

"Open the door, and get out of the way." Burt mentioned all precautions. A man with a gun and an attitude is not a very safe place. Tuck opened the door.

The patrol officer had passed Mayville and noticed headlights coming toward him, "Must be the tow truck. Guess I could call ahead to Steve and tell him it's on the way." The headlights pass him, "Yep, it's the tow truck. I'll give him a radio check." He turned on the radio and signaled for Steve.

"This is Highway Patrol 22, I hear ya!"

"Well, your tow truck is nearing Mayville. He just passed me."

"Ten-four! Thanks for the info. I thought you were keeping the radio off?"

"It was. I just decided to tell you about the tow truck."

"Thanks, again. This weather is getting pretty bad." The patrol officer then shut off his radio, seventeen miles from Hontra.

Mike Serby turned quickly toward the open door and fired! "Who goes there? You son-of-a-bitch! Who is it and what do you want?" Burt had left Tuck open the door, but he knew better than to show himself right away. Serby crouched down and maneuvered himself to see who, if anybody, stood outside the door, "Come on, you bastard! I've got a bullet waiting for ya! He steadied the gun and pointed it at the doorway.

Burt finally spoke, his insides turning, "Serby! It's just me, Burt! Mind if I come in?"

"Burt, you asshole! What you trying to do to me? Of course you can come in," Serby straightened up and started to walk toward the bar, gun by his side. Burt entered.

"Hey, how's it going, Serb?" Tuck and Simon stayed outside, crouched down next to the entrance.

"And what brings you out? You need a nightcap?" Serby lifted up a glass, half full, and drank it. "What would I do without this place, Burt? And Martha wants me to sell! Damn, what's with that!"

67

Burt slowly glided to the bar, letting Serby talk. The ladies approached Tuck and Simon outside. "Just be quiet," Simon instructed and the ladies listened. The wind howled as the snow pierced at their faces.

"Um," Burt tried to speak, "Why does she want you to sell?"

"She says it's engulfing me. She says it's the only thing I know, the only thing I care about!" Serby raises the gun in the air and brings it back down, leveling it with Burt's stomach. "Oh, how I want to pull this trigger! Why's she being such a bitch? Huh?"

"Calm down," Burt's sweating, trying to maintain. He swallows, "Hey, you got an extra drink?"

"Now you want a drink?" Serby looks at the bottles behind the bar. "What next asshole, my wife?" Serby turns back around, facing Burt, his eyes cold and sharp, his jaw tense. He brings the gun up from his side and uses it as a pointer, "Are you the reason she wants a divorce, Fatboy?"

Burt's arms rise, "Hey, I know nothing about it, man! Would you put that gun down, please?"

Serby lays the gun on the bar, "Uh, maybe you don't," he lifts his glass, now empty. "You say ya wanted a drink, Fatboy?"

"Uh, yeah, I'll have one," Burt gently walks over to Serby. "Quite the storm outside, huh?"

Serby grabs his glass, looks at Burt, and decides to pick his gun back up, "you don't know nothin' bout a stolen gun, do you?"

"No, I don't."

"Yeah, all right. Hard to trust anyone these days. I'll go fix us one," Serby strolls to the end of the bar, "still drinking with Jack, aren't ya?"

"That'll do it." Serby walks behind the bar and grabs the bottle off the shelf.

"So, what should I do? Divorce the bitch!" he pours a glass half full of whiskey. "You don't need ice, do you?"

"No, that'll be fine." Burt checks out the front door, still open. Then looks back to Serby, remaining silent and still.

"Hey, how's that door staying open? You brake the spring on it?" Serby lifts his gun and walks to the end of the bar, pass Burt, seeing if anything is out there. "You got something going on here, Fatboy?"

"No, Serb, just want a drink," Burt holds the expression of a happy man, but inside he's terrified.

"Well, I can't see nothing," Serby walks back to the glasses and adds soda. He puts them on the bar, sliding one to Burt. "Here you go! Should we have a toast to.......let's say, a toast to fatboys and bitches! How's that?"

"Uh, yeah. Sounds good. Here's to them." Burt raises his glass, while Serby stands on the other side of the bar, directly parallel, gazing at Burt. "Aren't you gonna join me?"

Serby starts to lift his glass, one hand on the gun. Burt holds his glass, waiting for the toast to be complete. Bang! Serby fires a shot across the room! "You son-of-a-bitch, you been sleeping with my old lady, haven't ya?"

"Holy shit, man! I haven't came close to her!" Tuck and Simon jumped when they heard the gunshot and entered the bar. The ladies jumped also, fearing the worst, but once they heard Burt's voice they grabbed each other, tightly.

"Now, who are these boys? They come here to save your ass, Fatboy?" Serby backed up from the bar and leaned against the back cupboard. "You have anymore surprises?" He pointed the gun back at Burt.

"No. I don't know what these guys are doing here."

"And isn't it funny how the door closed when they came in?" Burt froze. Tuck and Simon wanted to leave, but their feet were stuck. "Let me tell you something, Burt," Serby stepped forward. "Since you got something going with my old lady, I'll let you go, but as for me," he lifted the revolver head level, "one bullet for the werewolf!"

"No!! Don't do it!" Burt dove across the bar just as the blast went off. Mike Serby falls to the floor.

You come home from the county fair, stuffed animals and blue ribbons in tow, the phone rings, you answer it for your mother, you hand her the phone and watch. Tears begin to flow down her cheek, you sit bewildered. She hangs up the phone and reaches out to you, "your daddy. He's been in an accident."

The roller-coaster, we will call life. One moment you're on top and the next they're throwing dirt in your face. Lucky are the few who have someone to reach out to.

Burt crawled down from the bar to Serby's side. Pat rushed in as Tuck and Simon ran up to the bar. Becky and Kim followed behind Pat, very slowly. "No, Mike. Why?" Burt cried out. "Don't just stand there, call 911!!"

Tuck rushed to the phone. Simon corralled the ladies, "I don't know his condition."

"Whose? Burt's or Serby's?" Pat asked, confused.

"Serby shot himself," Simon embraced tightly.

"Let go of me!" Becky demanded and pulled away, "I'm going to be sick!" She ran out the door and bent over. Even though she didn't know Serby, it was the thought making her stomach turn.

"Mayville, Serby's Bar, there's been a shooting!" Tuck tried to maintain authority.

"I'll send an ambulance right away! But the weather might slow us down." The dispatcher stated, then radioed the hospital. Nineteen miles to Mayville. She also radioed for a Highway Patrol.

"They're coming, Burt! An ambulance is on it's way."

"It don't matter," Burt lay next to Serby, cradling him, "he's dead, man. He's dead!"

Pat covered her face and began to cry, Simon held her, resting her head on his shoulder. He gave a small prayer towards the ceiling. Kim watched, then turned and walked outside. Tuck hung his head upon his hands, resting on the bar, then looked up, "Are you sure he's gone?" Burt remained silent, his best friend becoming cold. Tuck took the few steps toward Pat and Simon, collapsing on their support.

"Highway Patrol 22, I hear you!"

"Yes, a possible shooting in Mayville. I need you there ASAP! No one else is receiving my signal."

"Yeah, all right," Remembering he told the other officer to shut off his radio. "We're hooking up the tow right now and I'll be on my way. Ten-four!"

"Are you going to be all right, Becky?" Kim asked.

"Ah, yes. I just can't take death," she turns toward Kim and falls into her arms, "it's so, so final."

"It's okay, Becky," Kim holds her, cares for her, "besides, the storm is over." The snow quit and the wind calmed down, a peaceful moon in the distance.

Smalltown, U.S.A., you'll find one in every core of a big city—don't be surprised! Everyday living sometimes cuts us short of our true intentions. We have bills and obligations just like any other Joe, kids to feed, nurture, and teach. It is up to us, guardians, parents, teaches, and siblings to keep the fire glowing, to keep the warmth in the family. But ever-so-often a brother or sister revolts against the truth, finding out for themselves what lays on the other side of the fence. Mike Serby busted, he now knows where evil lurks. Do yourself a favor and share in the blame.

The Highway Patrol pulled up first, flashers on. He opened his door and got out of the car. Kim, Becky, and Simon were outside standing next to the entrance, "He's in here!" The Highway Patrol followed. Burt still lay on the floor next to his buddy, hunting and fishing days gone by. Tuck had sat down with Pat, who wondered about Irvin, Mike Serby's nephew, and Martha, Mike Serby's wife.

"Okay!" the officer spoke for attention, "I'll need statements from all involved. Is their anyone in particular who can tell me the whole story?"

"Yes, officer, I can!" Tuck stood up. "Mike Serby's laying behind the bar with a shot to his head." Tuck pointed to the area, then strolled over to the bar. The officer followed. "Where's the ambulance?"

69

The officer looked over the bar, then back at Tuck, "It should be on it's way. Let's see if we can pick him up. Excuse me," he now directed his voice at Burt, "can I have a word with you?" Burt looked up, then back down at his friend. "He might be in shock!"

Pat walked over to the bar while Tuck and the officer went behind the walnut. Simon observed from a distance. Kim and Becky went back outside. As the officer knelt down beside Serby he heard sirens, "the ambulance is here! Can you help them?" he asked Tuck.

Tuck ran to the front door, while the officer tried to talk to Burt, "I'm only here to help. What is your name?"

"Burt Olsen, I'm his best friend." he squeezed Serby's shoulder.

The officer looked up at Pat, "Can you help me?"

"Yes," she started to come out of the fog. "What do you need?"

"Can you talk to him while we try to get this guy out of here," he noticed the ambulance crew entering the premises.

"Burt! Stand up for me, please," Pat begged. She repeated the words, again.

"It's all right, Burt, you can get up." The officer grabbed Burt's coat sleeve and stood up. The ambulance crew stood behind him. "He might be in shock." Burt finally let go of his best friend and slowly rose to his feet. "You okay?"

"Are you okay, Burt?" Pat reached out.

"Yeah, but that's my best friend!" Burt's eyes started to drop tears. "And now he's gone."

Pat grabbed a hold of Burt's coat, "Come here, you still have me."

The officer backed away from the scene, noticing Pat gently persuading Burt to the other end of the bar, so the ambulance personnel could check Mike Serby. "Anything?" one questioned.

"No, nothing. I'm sorry."

"We'll have to get the gurney in here." Pat continued to comfort Burt, who was slowly regaining composure. The ambulance personnel walked out to the ambulance, returning with the gurney, and a body bag. The officer pulled out a notepad and scanned for his first witness. Tuck stepped forward.

"My name's Tuck, Tuck Jones, I've been employed here the last two weeks. I'm sure you have some questions," he stood ready, honest, and complaisant. Simon stood behind him as Kim and Becky re-entered the bar. Pat and Burt seemed to be in their own little corner, looking away from Mike Serby, looking only at each other.

"Thanks, Mr. Jones, my name's Duggan, Officer Paul Duggan, and yes, I do have some questions," playing his part in a professional world, what happened, when did it happen, and for what reason(s). The questioning began, first Tuck, then Simon, Becky and Kim gave what little they had to offer, and then the officer walked over to Pat and Burt. Mike Serby is being lifted into the ambulance.

Burt notices the officer coming up behind Pat, "I think he wants to talk to us," he nods in the officer's direction. Pat acknowledges and turns sideways.

"Hi, Officer Duggan. I have a few questions."

"Okay," Burt takes a deep breath, out of the corner of his eye he notices the front door shut, Mike Serby is gone. "Yeah, I'm ready."

"Were you friends with the victim?"

"Yes, many years. We used to go fishing, hunting, and all that stuff."

"Used to? When was the last time you went out together?"

"I don't know. It's been a couple of years, but I still always came down here. It's sort of my second home." The officer takes notes and continues.

"Did he seem distant, lately? Any reason for his health or welfare?"

"Huh? I don't know what you mean."

"Did he bring up any problems, socially or family-wise?"

"No, not to me, anyway. He seemed the same as always."

"Friendly and talkative?"

"Yeah, he always wanted to talk."

"And what would he like talking about?"

"Things, the usual. He would talk about the weather, sports, current news. You know?"

The officer jotted down more notes, "Did he ever mention his family?" Burt paused, flipping through the dialogue in his memory.

70

"Not much, really."

"Okay, I think I have enough. And your name?" he questioned Pat.

"Um, Pat Conner," caught a little off-guard.

"Friend of Mike Serby?"

"You could say that. I come in here quite often," on the fidgety, don't-want-to-say-nothing-wrong mode. She knew some of Mike's habits, drinking too much, cocaine, and that affair thing he had.

"And your place tonight?" she gives a confused expression, "Where were you when Mr. Serby...." he nods his head down.

"Outside the door," she points to the front entrance. "I was outside."

"You were outside with the others," he points to Becky and Kim.

"Yes. I didn't come in until the second shot."

"Second shot? He shot more than once?" he looked at Burt.

"Yeah," shaking his head, "the first time he just shot, to scare me, I think."

"And why would he do this?" Tuck and Simon walked over, standing behind Pat, Burt still stood behind the bar, his back to the past. Becky and Kim went back outside, needing fresh air and a cigarette.

"I don't know! He was accusing me of cheating with his wife!" he puts his head into his hand.

"And were you?"

"No!" Burt yells out with no obstruction. "I had nothing to do with her."

Duggan observes his reaction and nods his head, "Okay, that's all I need. Thank you all for your cooperation. And can anybody lock this place up?"

"Yeah, I have the keys!" Tuck informs. Burt takes a giant step over a ghostly image, laying on the floor. Tuck notices, "do you have to mark the place?" he asks the Highway Patrol.

"Shoot, I guess I will. I'll just put yellow tape outside the building. He didn't have any business partners, did he?"

"No, not that I know of," Tuck answers, looking at Burt for assurance.

The Highway Patrol Officer notices no reaction from Burt, who's walking up to them, "Okay, guess the place will be closed. Thanks, again." He nods his head and exits through the front door.

Irvin had been kept in the control car while the officer entered the County Police Station. "Where have you been?" asked the radio dispatcher. "I've been trying to contact you!"

"I'm bringing in a suspect, DWI, and I didn't want to deal with interruptions."

"Oh, that's nice! You think you can just shut off your radio? Is that what you did?"

"Uh, yeah, what did I miss? I seen the ambulance."

"And you still kept your radio off? I'm sorry, but this will have to be reported!"

"So be it," he held other interests, and being a cop was getting to be boring, he thought. "Say, I'm wondering what I should do with this one, Mr. Baker. He might have experienced a concussion."

"Then take him to the hospital and get him tested! Man, how did you earn Sergeant?" The officer shrugged his shoulder and walked back out to the squad car. "Sheez!" A message was coming in from Mayville.

"Patrol 22, read me?"

"Ten-four, go ahead."

"I'm coming in. The shooting turned out to be a suicide, Mr. Mike Serby, owner of the town bar, 'Serby's'. I have statements from an employee and some associates of his, but his wife stayed in Minneapolis, whereabouts unknown. A Mr. Tuck Jones supplied me with most of the information, says Mike Serby's wife, Martha, brought up divorce at a wedding party. Guess he couldn't handle it."

"Ten-four, bring it in. The victim being transported?"

"Ten-four. Should be on his way to Hontra Hospital. Might as well keep him there until his wife gets notified. I'll try to locate her, somehow, or come back here, to Mayville, once I get the paperwork filed."

"Ten-four, 22. See you in a bit. How's the weather?"

The officer looked out his windshield, then opened his window, "That's funny, it's clear skies and calm." He sits for awhile, trying to recollect the evening. "What happened to the blizzard?"

71

Tuck made a walk-around, checking to be sure all the doors were locked. Simon had found a mop and bucket. Pat served herself and the other ladies a drink, they needed it, their nerves being shaken and their minds numbed. "This has been quite the day. I guess Mayville has changed," Kim uttered.

Pat looked up from her mixing, "No, this is just a strange coincidence."

"I call it fate," Simon interrupted, splashing the mop down on the floor, trying to erase the past. Burt stands by the window watching the squad car leaving down Main Street.

Irvin, still in handcuffs, entered the hospital with the patrol officer, "I need this guy checked out for a concussion, and also a blood test," the officer demanded to the desk nurse.

"You'll have to wait. Just have a seat over there." She left the desk and started checking the hallways for another nurse.

"How you doing?" the officer asked Irvin.

"Not bad. I could be lot better, though." The nurse reappeared.

"You can step right down this hallway and Nurse Ann will take care of you."

The officer stood up first, "come on, Baker." Irvin then stood up and followed.

Burt slowly walked over to the bar, sitting down next to Kim, "What a shame. How can a person do something like that?" Kim turned toward Burt, putting her hand on his shoulder.

"Sometimes, Burt, but not always, it's the only thing they have left." Burt stares into her eyes, confused. "They think they've given all they possibly could and the only thing they have left is leaving. Maybe he figured his wife would be better off without him."

"But he didn't have to kill himself!"

"Burt, it's the only way he could leave her." Burt falls into her arms and she holds him. Pat and Becky bend their heads down, a moment of silence. Simon stops at the end of the bar, before putting the mop and bucket back into the store room, and observes the giving. Tuck stands by the light switch, his last task before leaving. "I'm sure he'll be all right, in his own special place."

Simon pushes the mop and bucket into the store room. Tuck shuts off the lights, all but one, "We all ready?" he asks openly. Pat and Becky rise, physically silent and emotionally touched. Kim pushes Burt away softly, "come on, Burt! It's time we go." Burt looks up to Kim, his head hanging at half-staff, she touches the side of his face with her hand, in a brushing motion, and delivers a tear of her own along with a smile.

"Thank you, Kim," Burt rises, holding back from kissing her. She lets go in silence and collects herself, and she, too, rises. Simon and Tuck stand next to the door as the rest file out. The brisk air lifts them, the calm allows them to listen, and in the distance the moon and the stars show them light. "You all want to finish that Cribbage game?"

Pat cracks a smile, "You're silly."

"Um, I'm in!" Kim raises her hand.

"Cool! I'm glad you two came home!" Burt finds an extra hop in his step and leads the way. Tuck follows, the last in line, wondering how his life had been changing, and now, too, so would the people in front of him. He glanced at the skies, a distant cloud rolling toward them, a prayer is given.

The nurse had taken Irvin to a small examining room to take a blood test, she would then cart him down the hallway where a doctor would check him for a concussion. She now held the results, "Mr. Baker, you've been drinking quite heavily tonight. Your results are pretty high." She passed the paperwork to the officer. "Still want a concussion exam?"

"Yeah. Let's cover all the bases. I'll wait in the lobby, seems I got paperwork to fill out."

Pat silently caught up to Burt's hopping steps, "Burt, can I have a quick word with you?"

He stops, "Huh? What do you need?"

"I overheard something about divorce. Was that why...you know. Was that why he did what he did?" Pat's mind seemed full, a small piece of history bothering her, maybe involving her. The others stood a few steps from them.

"Yeah. He accused me of sleeping with Martha and wondered if that was why she wanted a divorce," Burt's comfort vanished, his anger and suspicion rose. Tuck stepped forward.

"He told me she wanted a divorce, but he never told me why. Maybe he was having one."

Pat held her head in her hand, and then looked at Burt, "That's what I mean. Maybe Tuck is right."

72

"Serby? Who would he be having an affair with?!" Tuck stepped back. Kim, Becky, and Simon stood as intrigue was about to unfold before them.

Pat takes a deep breath and delivers the message, unmasking the secret, "My mom, Burt. Her and Mike Serby were doing it."

"No way! Your mom?"

"Yes, and don't believe for a minute I'm happy about it. I told her not to get involved!"

"Oh, so you told her? Did you do anything else.....to stop it?" Burt closed the gap between himself and Pat to a few inches.

"And you're his best friend? Didn't he share any of this with you?" Pat fired back.

"No! Maybe your mom was just saying this shit! Are you even sure there was an affair?"

Pat paused and switched into neutral, "maybe not. I guess we're both wrong."

"Huh? Ah, what? So you're just saying this crap?"

Simon stepped in between the two accusers, "Hey, it's been a long night, I don't think either one of you is to blame for anything. Pat's mom, neither."

"Ah, what do you know?" Burt places his hand upon Simon's chest, then pushes off, "I don't need you guys coming over."

"Burt! It doesn't have to be anyone's blame, but his own!"

"Ah, you think whatever you want. The guy is married, Pat!" and Burt kept walking west down Main Street, his shelter waiting.

Simon places his hand upon Pat's shoulder, "He'll be all right. Tomorrow's another day, when he'll change his way."

"I hope so," Pat's face covered lightly with tears. "My mom tried to break things up."

Kim, Becky, and Tuck walked toward Pat, "You mind if me and Simon stop over at your place?"

"Not at all, Tuck. Matter of fact, I'd appreciate the company."

"And what are we?" Becky with hands on hips.

"Come here, friend! We're going to have a good time, yet!"

"Well, Mr. Baker," the doctor informed, after a brief examination, in which he pushed on Irvin's skull, looked into his eyes, and checked for reaction and reflex, "all I can tell you is to watch yourself. If you become nauseated, dizzy, maybe a slight memory loss, I would like to see you come back in. But for now, I'm going to hold off from taking any x-rays. Okay?"

"I guess," Irvin shrugs his shoulders. The doctor leaves the room and a nurse soon enters.

"Guess I'll lead you back to the lobby. You're escort is waiting."

"Yeah," Irvin pictured a nice cot in a one-man cell.

The group decided to head south down First Avenue, leaving their vehicles behind, "It's turned into a nice night for a stroll, after all," Pat remarked. "Too bad the bakery's not open!" as they strolled by the front window of 'Claire's Home Bakery'.

"It is a beautiful night, but donuts? You're silly, Patty!" Kim enticed. The ladies started to giggle, their thoughts of now. They walked away from earlier events and held no expectations for the future, they laughed for the moment.

"Ya know, Tuck, they're pretty cool! Aren't they?" Simon smiles, enlightening Tuck on the simple facts of life—forgive, forget, and laugh a lot. Observe the beauty in action and respect it with a smile, the only ingredient necessary.

"Yeah, I guess."

Simon backhands him in the chest, frowning with his eyebrows, "Loosen up, boy! You're in Mayville, not St. Cloud."

"Huh?" Tuck's mind wondered to the shared laughs he had with his ex-wife, such an entertaining noise pulling at his heart strings, then he caught on to what Simon meant. "I'm trying, man. Yesterday was the eighteenth month anniversary of our divorce."

"Hey, one year's the limit, then you quit celebrating!"

"Hey, look guys!" Kim exclaimed, "It's beginning to snow, again!"

Some people put their hands in their pockets to keep them warm, some people put their hands in their pockets to feel the coins, make the noise, some people put their hand in one pocket only to pull something out.

Can you make change for a dollar? Is it the coins they are after or is it a helping hand they are ready to give? Don't feel the pressure, rather accept the gift.

"Found 'em!" a brief search for her keys in a small purse, but a full purse, and Pat inserted the tool necessary to get in, "shelter at last!"

"All right!" Becky exclaimed, getting a little on the freeze side. She is only wearing a skirt. "I hope you have the heat on." The door opens and the entrance is made. Pat lays her keys on the table next to the door.

"Anyone for a drink?" asked out of habit. "I have some booze in the kitchen."

"Yeah, I'll have one," Kim admits.

"Me, too," Becky follows, then turns to Tuck, "Do you like snow?"

"Uh, yeah, sort of. What kind of snow?" It's the way she asked.

"Mirrors and straws," in a cute whisper, the kind wanting trouble.

Tuck fell earlier to pressure, or is it taste, and now a cute, firm, wanting little piece-of-ass, "I had some earlier." The anniversary barely hangs in his mind, a beginning stands right before him.

"And what's earlier?" she smiles.

"Uh, yeah, I'll have some. If you have any, that is."

"Of course I do," she punches him on the shoulder. "You want to ask Pat if she wants any?"

Simon takes off his coat and lays it on the couch separating the living room and dining room. He then walks into the kitchen. Kim and Pat are already in the kitchen, Pat lifting up bottles from the bottom cupboard and Kim reaching for glasses. "Gin, Vodka, or Whiskey?"

"Gin, my dear. Hey, Simon, you drinking tonight?"

"No thanks. Gotta keep the pact."

Pat heard his comment, but rather not get into a counter—counter point. "Gin, it is!" She put the other two bottles back down and stood up, twisting off the cap. "The tonic water is in the fridge and I have no limes."

"No limes?" A weeping cry from Kim.

"But, I do have lime juice!" Simon nodded his head and left the kitchen, taking a seat at the dining room table. Becky and Tuck had removed their coats, throwing them on the couch. Tuck joined Simon at the table while Becky walked on into the kitchen, "Hey, Beck, ready for a Gin-Tonic?"

"Yes I am. And how about some cocaine?"

"You still have some?"

"Yes I do, and Tuck said he would like some."

Burt had entered his domain, tipped over the make-shift box and all the cards on top of it, turned on the stereo, cranking up the volume, then taking a seat in his favorite chair. He reached under the chair and pulled out a tray, his tray, fully equipped with a so-called toolbox. Inside this toolbox: rolling papers, one-hitter, pipe, pipe-cleaner, and private stash. "Time for toast. Screw everyone! Serby, this one's for you."

He took a pinch of marijuana and stuffed it into his pipe, noticed a lighter on the floor, must've been on the box, picked it up, and lighted the green, with a little red, bud.

Tuck sat across from Simon at the oblong table, "So, what do you think?"

"I don't know. Just let it happen, I guess," Simon reflected. Becky came back into the dining room carrying a small mirror, it had been tucked away in Pat's junk drawer.

"Here, Tuck. Want to do the honors. Three lines, unless...." she looks down to Simon.

"No thanks, I've had my fun."

"Okay, three lines." She then struts back into the kitchen.

"Just let it happen," Tuck comments. Simon shifts his head. "But all I have is a mirror," he picks it up, turning it from side to side.

"Well, use it. Maybe she's telling you something."

"Oh, here, Tuck," Becky re-enters, "I forgot to give you the snow!"

74

"Uh, thanks," unsure of her true intentions. Was his hair messed up, was their something on his face, or did she just set him up to see how foolish he acted? "And a razor blade?"

She curtsies from the neck up, "I'm being so forgetful, I'm sorry." She leaves, back into the kitchen. Tuck tries to hold his facial color, but the blush is peeking out. Simon covers his grin, but can't help himself from watching the colors turn brighter. "Here, this'll work, Tuckie.." She slides a small utility knife across the table, smiling all the way. Tuck reaches for it as she keeps sliding it closer, until the flesh of their fingertips touch. She holds the moment, taking a picture with her eyes.

"Well, Mr. Baker, here needs to be booked and bunked." The officer pushes the paperwork to the desk sergeant. "As you can see," he points to the blood test, "he's had quite enough."

"Okay, we'll take care of him." Irvin took a seat, blank-minded, and why not, his nightmare had just begun.

"Say, whatever happened with the ambulance call?"

"Suicide. Duggan should be pulling in here, anytime. He was gonna try to locate relatives, but no such luck, yet."

"Hmmm, crazy night, huh? Well, I'm checking out. They said I could have half the night off, and I'm taking it!" Irvin heard the conversation, the voices, but made no sense of it. His mind remained incoherent, depressed, and all alone.

Kim and Pat entered the dining room, Pat taking the seat on the far end and Kim taking the seat on the near end, to Simon's left. "Look at all of this stuff!" Kim remarked, shoving a pile of envelopes to the side, next to Tuck.

"What?" Pat demanded. "Like, you don't have bills? Tuck, did you want anything to drink? How about you, Simon?"

"I'm just kidding," Kim gives a grin. "Can I put them on the floor?"

"Yeah, go ahead. You two want anything?"

"Goathead!" Kim recalls the namesake. Her and Pat share a giggle.

"Uh, I'll have plane soda. If you have one?" Tuck answers.

"Water's fine with me," Simon follows.

Pat then looks at the mirror in Tuck's possession, "Hey, want to mix and match?" Becky enters the room and sets her glass down between Kim and Simon.

"Huh? Mix and match?" Tuck questions. Becky walks halfway around the table and straight down the hallway.

"I'll add some smoke to the fire. Here," Pat slides the mirror over to herself, "you have it pretty well cut up. Kim, can you get these two something to drink?" She gets up from the table and walks over to the couch, where her coat and purse were thrown, "Say, who wants to play DJ?" She picks up her purse, opens it, and takes out the bag of weed.

"I will!" Simon reacts to her question. "What you want to hear?"

"You're the DJ. Pick and choose."

Pat struts back to the table, takes her seat, and becomes a chemist, "You mix," she holds up the mirror, "and I match," she holds up the baggie. "Shit! We don't have any papers."

Tuck reaches into his pocket, "Yeah we do!" and pulls out the wrappers.

Burt had taken a few hits, closed his eyes, and went off to another world. The music still played at high volume, adding to his kaleidoscope dream. Drifting away from the night's contortions and melodramas, along with the accusations and misconceptions. His body and mind relaxed as if floating on a cloud, destination unknown, destination ignored.

Kim sets down two glasses, "One water for Simon and one soda for Tuck," she slides them to the respectable recipients. Once a waitress, always a waitress. She then takes her seat as Becky enters from the hallway, having had to use the bathroom. "So, now what?" After a few minutes of crowd observation, Simon settles on the music. The first CD begins to spin. (insert your favorite crowd pleaser)

"Okay, Mr. Baker," finger prints had been taken and the camera buzzed, "look at the light, hold your number chest high. That's it!" click, "Okay, now turn to your side, hold your number above the elbow. That's it!" click, "And one more shot. Turn, facing the opposite direction. Hold your number above the elbow. That's it!" Click. "Okay, next stop is pillows and sheets. Leave the number on the table."

75

"I'll roll this up, and, Kim why don't you get a deck of cards out of the junk drawer." Pat's house, Pat's instruction. Kim leaves the table and goes into the kitchen.

"What we gonna play?" Becky asks.

"We'll see when the card's get here," Pat sprinkled the weed on the paper. Tuck and Simon remained silent, observant. Kim enters the room with a deck of cards.

"Here you go! Now what?"

"Take the cards out of the package," Pat sprinkles a little powder on top of the weed. Kim takes the cards out of the package.

The table is set, music plays, treats are soon to be lighted up, and the contestants sit in their ready position. From the head of the table, where Pat is positioned, and going clockwise. Next to Pat sits Simon, then Becky. Kim sits at the other end of the table and Tuck is to her left. "Should I shuffle them?"

"Definitely! Anyone have a light?" Pat holds up the treat.

"Okay, Mr. Baker, one pillow, one sheet, and one blanket," Irvin grabs the order. "Next stop will be your last, cell number seven. Must be your lucky number, huh?" Irvin hangs his head at half-staff, his mind numb, as he follows his feet.

"Now what?" asks Kim, "I've shuffled them five times."

"Deal out seven cards to each of us," Pat takes the lighter from Tuck, then sparks the joint. Kim begins to disperse the cards. Becky watches Tuck across the table, not staring, just a little peek-a-boo. Simon relaxes, "what happens, happens."

"Huh? What the....?" Burt wakes up to a knock at the door. "Who is it?" he yells, while trying to get up from his chair.

"Police Officer. I have some questions."

"Oh, shit. Yeah, I'll be right there." Burt picks the pipe off the floor, puts it on the tray, and slides it under his chair. He grabs the can of air freshener and sprays, while on the way to the door. He tosses the can to the side and opens the door.

"Sorry to disturb you, but do you know how I could get in contact with any of Mike Serby's family?" spoken quick, it had been a long night.

"She's not home?" Burt still carried cobwebs in his brain.

"No. I've been waiting for quite awhile. Do you know if she stayed out of town for the night?"

"Don't know. All I know is what I saw."

"Any ideas on who else I could talk to? Maybe a brother, sister, nephew...."

"Yeah, his nephew. Irvin Baker!"

The name sounds familiar, "Irvin Baker? And what's the relationship?"

"That's Serby's nephew. Lives about eight, nine miles out of town. He was in town earlier."

The name catches, "Irvin Baker? Does he drive a silver and blue pick-up, S-10?"

"Yeah, that's him."

"Thanks. I know exactly where he is." the officer turns, but Burt stops him.

"Hey, where is he?"

"Hontra! We busted him about two hours ago."

Simon passed on the smoke, but Becky enjoyed it, taking a long drag and holding it in. Kim finished dealing out the cards and set the pile in the middle of the table, "Now what?"

"Smoke this," Becky handed her the joint.

"Crazy Eight, silly!" Pat answered. "Tuck, you start." Kim choked on the inhale.

"Crazy Eight? You're silly!" Kim took another hit and passed the joint to Tuck.

Tuck had picked up his cards, "Thanks," he said to Kim, taking the joint from her. He takes a hit and passes it on to Pat. "So, we're playing Crazy Eight?" Smiles and nods around the table.

"Why not?" Pat smirks. "Now, Tuck, lead out!" Tuck follows her instruction and drops down the ace of spades. "Ace of spades." she sounds off in a deep voice and takes a drag off the joint. Kim and Becky laugh, relating her remark to a past episode. "Here Simon."

Simon takes the joint, second guesses, and takes a small hit. He then passes it on. Pat lays down the ten of spades. Simon follows with the ten of diamonds. Pass the joint, lay down a card, pass the joint, lay down a card—pretty crazy......

"Mr. Baker, one more time before I lock you up. Are you sure you don't want to make a telephone call?" the question is met with uncertainty and shame written within lonely eyes, "Okay."

Going off to college, scholarship in hand, you have waited, you have prac-
ticed, and you have earned it. Recruited from the big schools, to you they
were. Who would have ever thought you would be noticed from such a
small town. But it happened and your parade is waiting. On the inside
you have just conquered a Lifetime Achievement.

In a moment's notice, the time it takes for you to hear the phone ring
three times and have you answer with a 'hello', your scholarship turns into
hardship. Your parents are gone, not a pretty accident, leaving you with
responsibility and the farm. The decision is yours.

"I can't believe we're playing this!" Tuck spoke his mind, not being
accustomed to childish games.

"Just shut! No one else had any ideas, so we're playin'. Now, who's turn
is it?" Pat commanded. The joint made it's final lap as Tuck put the roach
on the edge of the ashtray. "Kim, lay a card."

"I hope this Serby thing gets taken care of," Simon feeling sincere, "I
mean, he does deserve family."

"Huh?" Becky questioned his wording.

"In other words," Kim cut in, "no one deserves to be alone. Right,
Simon?"

"Yeah," Simon glowed.

"And, Simon," Pat asked, throwing down the Queen of Hearts,
"where's your family?"

"For now," Simon said readily, "they're right around this table," he gave
a sweeping motion with his arm.

"Isn't that nice?" Becky didn't understand, she really didn't want to.

"He means well," Kim plays mother, "Simon, anyone tell you how giving you are?"

"Uh, I don't get into that," Simon blushed and laid down the eight of diamonds, "I change it to diamonds," as he points to the discarded eight.

"You shit! I don't have any diamonds," Becky starts picking up from the pile. "Can't we play something else?"

"Right after this hand," Tuck takes the lead, "Simon'll show us some of his games."

Burt had walked through the living room, giving the box on the floor one more kick, and sauntered down the hallway to his bedroom. He pulled his sweatshirt off, undid his jeans and threw them on the floor, then crawled beneath the covers of his twin-bed. "Tonight has got to be a dream, just a dream," he shuts his eyes, putting out the scenes of reality.

The bars slammed behind him as he now stands in a dimly lit cage. Silence becomes a lonely noise. Irvin throws his pillow and bedding on the small cement shelf, intended for his body, "I'm sorry dad," he looks up to the bare ceiling, "I really did it this time." He sits next to his pillow and folds his hands, bowing his head, "I hope your listening, I need your help. It's not that I do these things on purpose, my Lord, but I'm so confused. Please, help me. Please, tell me what to do." He sits in the silence, tightly grasping his hands, eyes shut. He then lets go.......

Pete and Donna had shared one last joint a few hours earlier and lay cuddled together under a stack of warm blankets, big Sampson lay on the floor next to the bed, and Burnie, the black and white Tomcat, all fifteen pounds of him, lay at the foot of the bed. Mike Serby had been carted down the stairs of the hospital, waiting for relative recognition. His wife, Martha, who stayed in Minneapolis with her sister, now wondered, as they sat at the kitchen table, "Maybe I should call home."

"It's up to you," her sister, Kate, did not hold back.

"I don't know. I just feel guilty about the whole situation. The way I mentioned divorce in front of all those people."

"You had it all built up inside," Kate informed, "it was bound to happen sooner or later. I, for one, have been wondering how you two managed to stay together this long."

"I know. It's just......."

"You don't want to be the bad guy, right?"

"Uh, yeah, I guess," more of a cop-out than a straight answer. "Where am I sleeping, tonight?"

"Right down the hallway, second bedroom to your right. Have a good sleep."

77

Simon, holding three cards, decided on whether to match the suit of clubs with his ten or change the direction. Becky held one card. "Okay, I'll lay the eight of spades, and change it to.....diamonds!"

"I win!" Becky lays down the seven of diamonds. "Way to go, Simon!"

"One more game," Pat did not like to lose, no matter what the game.

"Nope! We agreed to play something different. Simon, what's next?" Tuck delegated with a smile.

Pat gave him a non-pleasing look, but kept her silence as she threw her cards into the middle of the table. Kim and Becky glanced at Simon, waiting for his answer. Tuck organized all the cards into a neat pile and handed them to Simon.

"Since I left 'The Edge' at the bar I'll have to say 'Characters'."

"'Characters'? I never heard that one," Tuck questioned.

"I haven't put it completely together, yet, but it is rather simple."

"How do we play?" Becky's mood consisted of eager, spontaneity, and willingness.

"How about a few drinks first?" Pat puts the action on pause.

"Yeah, I'll have a refill," Becky answers. Kim holds her glass up and also agrees.

Pat stands up from the table and walks into the kitchen, picking up Becky's and Kim's glasses along the way. Simon takes the opportunity to re-think the game's purpose and instructions. Tuck leaves the table for a bathroom break. The music continues to play.

"Simon, what kind of game is it?" Becky leans close, as if trying to get an advantage.

"Can't rightly say. It just sort of came to me."

"You can't tell us any secrets about it?" Becky glances back at Kim, still trying to get an edge.

"Nope. The only secrets to this game are your own," Simon shuffles the cards. "You'll see."

"Oh, oh, Beck, are we in trouble," Kim states forward.

"Whatever, let's just play the game! Haven't you got those cards dealt out, yet?"

"You on powder, or what?" Simon retaliates.

"Mmm, you should know," she pats her hand down on Simon's thigh and squeezes, while holding onto a thick smile.

"Uh, yeah, I remember. Here, let me deal out the cards." Becky backs off and shares a giggle with Kim. Pat and Tuck enter the dining room from opposite directions. Pat sets down the glasses as Tuck takes his seat. "Sorry, Pat, but could I get another glass of water?"

"You know where it is, but I'll get it."

"You figure it out, Simon?" Tuck questions, then takes a sip of his soda.

"He says there's no secrets," Becky pouts.

"Only your own," Simon re-informs.

"Ohh, secrets? This could be a night to remember," Tuck comments.

"I hope so," as Becky flashes a whisper across the table. Kim glances toward Simon, meeting his eyes head-on, and shares a smile. Pat sets down a glass of water for Simon.

"Tuck, you need more soda?" she asks before sitting herself down.

"No, I'm fine. Only need so much of this," he lifts his glass, setting it back down without taking a drink. "I've only been drinking it all day!"

Simon continues dealing out the cards as Pat takes a seat, "Okay, object of the game, there is none."

"Huh?" Pat wasn't sure she heard it right.

"Well, sort of. Let me finish dealing out the cards."

"You can't do two things at once?" Pat questions.

"No!" Becky supplies the answer.

"Uh, okay now," he lays down the last card, "you ready?"

"We've been!"

"Don't look at any of your cards and stack them in a nice pile," Simon organizes his own. "Like this. Then we play it just like 'High-Card', but different."

"So, we don't play it like 'High-Card'?"

"Well, sort of. Remember, I've never played it yet! We all throw a card down in the middle of the table," Simon throws in the King of spades. "Okay, Becky, throw in a card." She throws in the

78

two of hearts. "And Kim," She throws in the five of hearts. "Tuck? And so on," he motions to Pat. Tuck lays out the three of spades and Pat follows with the ten of diamonds.

"Now what?"

"High card wins, but there's a catch," Simon notices he has the high card. "Depending on the color, red or black, you mention something about yourself."

"Huh?" Becky reacts as if shocked by an unexpected guest.

"Here. I won, so I get to share," Simon demonstrates. "The King is high card and it's black," he points out. "Black means a good thing and red means a not-so-good thing. Oh, and is there Jokers in the deck?" he looks to Pat.

"Should be."

"When you get a Joker, you automatically win, but the rules change."

"And how's that?" Tuck keeps the thought moving.

"When you lay a Joker, be it red or black, everyone else gets to take a shot at you."

"Bullshit!" Becky straightens up in her chair, "I'm not playing this."

"Come on," Kim pushes, "what have you to hide?" The CD player stops.

"Okay, Simon, tell us a good-thing," Pat pushes forward, noticing Becky's reaction.

"A good thing about myself. I like to help others."

"That's it? You like to help others."

"Yeah, no one said how deep you gotta go. Next card," Simon lays out the two of diamonds, Becky follows with the four of clubs, Kim with the four of hearts, Tuck with the ten of hearts, and Pat lays down the nine of spades. "Tuck, you're call."

"Oh, oh," Becky flirts across the table, "it's a red one!"

Tuck smiles at the thought, "no, I can't say that. Let's see, a bad thing about myself.....I get angry at little things."

"So you're touchy?" Pat reaches over and pokes him in the ribs.

"Hey, I'll knock your head off!" He laughs as Pat sits back, a little surprised, then she, too, begins to laugh. "I'm just kidding. But I can get upset over nothing, ask my ex-wife."

"Okay," Simon tries pushing the train forward, not wanting Tuck to get stuck in the past, "next card." Simon lays out a six of spades. Becky lays a Queen of hearts, Kim lays a nine of diamonds, Tuck throws down a three of hearts, and Pat lays down a seven of clubs. "And the winner is Becky!"

"Oh shit!"

"And it's a bad thing," Tuck returns the gesture.

"Hearts should be a good thing, don't you think?" Putting off the interrogation or simply a suggestion for the game.

"Yeah, Simon, hearts are good," Kim sided with Becky.

"Vote on it! All for red is bad, black is good raise their hand," Simon raises his hand, the only one to do so. "Okay, red is good and black is bad."

"Wait a minute," Pat interrupts, "maybe we should categorize. I mean, this is a new game, right?"

"Yeah, so feel free to critique," Simon accepted her idea. "How should we categorize?"

"Instead of going with red and black why not go with the different suits."

"Okay, hearts is good!" Becky mentions with zeal.

"Deeper than that," Pat informs.

"Oh, oh, Becky, here we go," Kim leans toward her.

"What's it going to be?" Tuck asks impatiently.

"Hearts are for good things," Pat suggests.

"All right!" Becky raises her arm.

"But not only good things, but things you love," Pat scans the table for approval, "diamonds are things you like to spend money on."

"Another good thing!" Becky's alive.

"Just chill. Spades are things you like to do and clubs are places you like to visit. Sound cool?" Pat can't believe the accomplishment.

"Yeah, sounds cool. Maybe we should write this down," Simon agreed.

Pat stands up from the dining room table and walks over to the small table next to the door, "It's really snowing out there!" Simon gets up from the dining room table and walks over to her.

79

"Here, I found a notepad." She hands Simon the notepad, it looks like the one Officer Duggan carried. "And here's a pencil."

"Thanks, I wonder if Serby's wife ever found out?"

"Oh, Simon, don't ruin this for me," Pat hid her true feelings about the night and she rather not let them out. "And don't you dare bring up Irvin."

"I won't," Simon apologized. They both went back to the dining room table. Kim, Becky, and Tuck were dissecting categories. "Say, what happened to the tunes?" Pat went back to the stereo.

"So, hearts are giving, diamonds are spending, spades are things to do, and clubs are places to go?" Tuck asked for assurance.

"Yep, and the Joker plays the bad guy!"

"Oh, you!" Becky thought the 'bad thing' was dismissed.

"There's got to be something bad."

"Should we roll another joint?" Tuck speaks up and reaches into his pocket.

"I'm for that," Becky gasps.

"Where did you get the smoke?" Simon wonders.

"I'm not telling. It's a small town," Tuck shrugs his shoulders, "and I'm a bartender. Pat, you have them papers?"

She pushes a few buttons and the CD player activates (insert your favorite song), "Sure do, right there on the floor!" She points under her chair. "While you do that, I'm gonna get out of this dress."

"And I'm taking a bathroom break," Simon adds.

Tuck reaches under the chair and brings up the papers, along with a mirror. He leaves Pat's baggie on the floor. "Anymore of this?" He holds the mirror up to Becky.

"A little. You sure you want anymore?"

"Nah, guess not," he read her expression. Tuck spills the contents of marijuana on the table and starts to siphon through it, "this'll do just fine."

Becky slides the notepad in front of her, Kim watches her, and then grabs the pencil, "What should I draw? A monkey or a squirrel." Kim and Tuck laugh. "I'm serious."

"Since when?" Kim keeps laughing. Tuck gives a serious look toward Becky, trying to figure her out, and then Becky, too, begins to laugh. "Don't even try, Tuck. Don't even try!" Kim warns. Tuck blushes and starts to roll, getting a little warm.

"What you drawing?" Simon asked as he entered from the hallway.

"Nothin'!" Becky exclaimed, a little off-guard. "Maybe we should change the name of the game since we changed the instructions. What do you think?"

"And what would you call it?" Pat asks, now wearing sweat pants and an extra-large football jersey. "My own little world."

"All right, Cardinals!" Tuck notices the logo on her jersey, "that's my team!"

"No, Patricia, I would not call it 'My World'. I don't know what I would call it."

"No fighting allowed!" Kim plays referee, "how about 'Strangers'?"

"Please describe," Simon sits down. He likes the name, but knows there has to be an explanation behind it. "Why 'Strangers'?"

Kim takes a deep breath and exhales, "All the suits represent a characteristic, right?"

"Yeah," Simon agrees. Tuck lights up the joint. Becky and Pat listen to the background.

"The person with the high card explains that characteristic to the others, right?"

"True, go on," Simon supports the description. Pat takes a hit off the joint and passes it to Simon. He takes it and passes it on to Becky, withdrawing from the smoke.

"And who are we telling these things to?" Becky takes a hit and passes the joint to Kim, "Thanks."

"Strangers?" Pat implies. Kim takes a long drag from the joint, passes it on to Tuck, and begins to cough. "Too much."

"Uh," Kim coughs, again, "what do you think?"

"You don't like 'Characteristics'?" Simon pleas.

"It's too long!" Becky adds her opinion.

"When's the last time you ever said that?" Kim remarks and the whole table erupts in laughter, including Becky.

They sleep, eat, groom themselves, and take care of their own offspring. Humans are very special in God's creation.

Animals are much the same, they are the same. Can you really tell me a difference? If you say they don't speak, how then do we recognize a bird's location. Sometimes animals are more human than we ourselves, at least they think that way—have you ever watched a monkey?

Becky takes her pile of cards and sets them in front of Simon, "Here, deal them over."

"Yeah, right. Just so you get out of saying anything?" Simon sensed her motive.

"No. We're starting a new game," she reaches across Simon and takes the joint from Pat. "We renamed it, so we gotta start over."

"Whatever," Simon shakes his head, "give me your cards and I'll re-shuffle."

"Becky, you're such a bitch," Kim offers the adjective. "Give me that stick!" She takes the joint from Becky, laughing. Simon rounds up the cards from around the table and re-shuffles.

"Are we going to write the rules down?" Tuck didn't want to start over, again.

"Yeah, I have the notepad, so give me the rules," Becky as Miss Important Secretary.

"Rule one," Kim starts, "no one leaves the table."

"That's not a rule," Becky refuses to write it down.

"Okay, then I'm going to the bathroom," Kim stands up and squeezes between Tuck and the wall. "When you gotta go, you gotta go."

"Tuck, what's another rule?" Becky continues.

"Hearts are giving," he demonstrates with his hand language, "diamonds are spending, spades are things to do, and clubs are places to go. You got that?"

"Yes," even though she was still on diamonds.

"Well, now we have two roaches on the ashtray," Pat places the butt of the joint next to the first one. "Unless, of course, someone's going to eat them?"

"I will," Simon accepts.

"You're weird. You wouldn't smoke anymore, but you're going to eat them?"

"Hey, I may be strange, but not weird! There is a difference," Simon recalls the childish chants which were aimed at him, just because of donning his first pair of glasses.

"Sorry, didn't mean to get you all riled up," Becky apologizes.

"That's okay, just a haunting from my past." He begins to deal out the cards, "and remember the Joker," his eyes float in Becky's direction.

"You wish, Simon, but it's not gonna happen."

"Pat, you have any munchies?" Tuck's stomach started to talk.

"Yeah. Becky, you want to get the bag of pretzels above the stove? And there's also peanuts and redhots in the second drawer down, way to the right," Pat's stomach must've been talking with Tuck's. Kim came back from the bathroom and squeezed back to her chair. Simon finished dealing out the cards and picked up a roach.

"You're not going to eat that, are you?" Kim playing mother.

"Uh," as if he had been caught in the cookie jar, "no. Just looking at it."

"Are you going weird?" Kim asked, while Tuck and Pat busted out with laughter. Simon nodded his head and placed the roach back on the ashtray. Becky came back to the table, setting the pretzels between her and Simon, the peanuts she slid over to Pat, and the redhots found a nice little space right in front of her.

"You can't have all of them!" Pat reaches for the redhots.

"Just wait. I'll pass them around."

"We're ready to start. Who's first?" Simon playing conductor.

"Like it matters," Becky lowers his position. "We all just throw a card!" They do just that. Cards in the air! Some on the floor, while others landed on the edge of the table, in the middle of the table, and one next to the bag of pretzels. "Guess it's yours, Simon. Your game, your story."

"No, no. Not all mine. You were the ones to rename it and give it detail, remember?"

"Ah, so it's not all yours," Becky with a puppy-face. "So, when you market it we all get a share?"

81

"Shhh, you are good," Simon knew a con, "but you have the right. This game belongs to all of us."

"Ooh, girl, you done that real good," Kim comments, "and you never wanted to be my agent?"

"Competition, Kim. I thought I was better than you."

"That's cool. Competition only made me better. Thanks for bringing it out," Kim knew herself and the limits she could put on her friends, an ability that lost her marriage.

"Okay, let's try it, again," Simon paused the sarcasm. "There, I have the ten of hearts."

Becky looked down and nodded her head, then abruptly raised her head, throwing out a card, "there, the Queen of diamonds!" Kim followed with the nine of spades, Tuck threw out the four of clubs, and Pat laid down the three of clubs. "Looks like I get the prize," keeping her focus straight ahead. "And diamonds, something I like to spend money on. I would have to say cocaine!"

Kim cringed, but made it unnoticeable to the others. Pat's eyes widened, "You go, girl!" Tuck and Simon kept their expressions hidden. "Next round." Pat throws out the King of spades, "Oh, Daddy!"

Simon flips his top card over and places it down in the middle of the table, "eight of spades." Becky follows with a ten of diamonds, Kim throws down the five of hearts, and Tuck flips over a Joker! "You got it, Tuck."

"What happens when you have the Joker?" Tuck asks.

"Everyone takes a shot at ya," Pat informs. "And I don't like the way you smell!"

"Oh, man," Tuck is not ready for this.

"And your legs are bowlegged!" Simon chimes in.

"I don't really know you," Kim states, "but, you mix a lousy drink."

"Come on, I'm the best," Tuck supports himself.

"Well, I think you're cute," Becky closes out the shooting match. (stop reading and take a look in the mirror).

"Six thirty breakfast!" the deputy yelled out to his three customers, setting the food trays one by one on a small ledge for the accused.

"Uh," Irvin rubbed his eyes, his head feeling slightly numb, except for a headache over his right eye, "morning." Time to face reality.

"Irvin Baker, front and center," the deputy called out.

"Yeah," Irvin tried waking up, "right here."

"Come on out, time for a breath test and a phone call," the deputy ordered.

"Phone call," as if he wanted to make one, "I wonder what time it is."

Irvin straightened out his hair with his fingers, taking a quick glance in the mirror, and walked out from his private cell.

"How ya feeling?" the deputy asked.

"Do you know what time it is?" shaking off the stupid question.

"Yeah, it's 6:30 a.m. Let's see if we can get you out of here."

"Sounds good to me, I got cows waiting."

The deputy opened the gate leading into the booking section of the jail, he then locked it up behind them. Escorting Irvin to a seating section the deputy directed Irvin to take a seat. The deputy walked over to a small room and came back with a breathalyzer device, "If you blow beneath a

.05 we can let you out on your own, otherwise we'll let you make a phone call." He handed the device to Irvin.

Irvin checked out the device and followed orders. The deputy observed as Irvin blew into the tube, which was attached to a small box, a calculating meter.

"Time's up," the deputy takes the device from Irvin and checks the results. "Not enough. The phone is located on the wall right over there," he points at it's location.

Irvin mopes over to the phone, thinking about who to call and what to tell them, while feeling like a damp mop, an ugly figure. He picks up the receiver and realizes, "I don't need any change."

"I have to stretch," Pat stands up from her chair, "how long have we been playing this game, anyway?"

Simon looks down at his watch, seeing the time and subtracting, "about three hours."

"Three hours! Oh, man, no wonder I'm getting stiff. Aren't you guys getting tired?" Pat yawns.

82

Kim stands up and joins the stretching. Becky starts to regroup all the cards, "we gonna play another round?"

"I don't think so," Pat answers. "I'm going to bed. You guys do whatever, but I need some shut-eye." She walks away from the table towards the front door, looking out the small window, "It has really snowed, guys!" Tuck and Simon stand up and trot over to Pat. Becky notices the game is over and walks into the kitchen, one more drink. "So, Tuck, you gonna shovel my sidewalk?"

"Now? Heck it's still snowing," Tuck dodged the situation. He loved the snow, but his back did not. At the same time, when a girl asks for a favor you listen.

"I'm just kidding! I'll get to it later," Pat smiles as she gives him a punch to the shoulder, "but for now, I'm going to bed!"

"Should we leave?" Tuck asks out of politeness.

"I don't care, but you can stay," Pat's house is her guests as well as her own.

"What do you think, Simon?" Tuck's feeling unsure.

"We can stay. No work until tomorrow." Simon shrugged his shoulders and sways back to the dining room table, "Thanks, Pat. Have a good sleep."

"I will!" Pat disappears down the hallway, far bedroom to the left.

"So now what?" Tuck asks, slowly moving back to the dining room table, then taking a seat.

"Munchies are gone," Kim implies. "I feel liking diving on that couch, myself."

"Oh, so just me and Simon?"

"And me!" Becky enters from the kitchen, fresh drink in hand. Tuck shines, a rather mystique glow, as he smiles from ear to ear.

"You guys have fun, I've made up my mind." Kim stands up and strolls into the living room, pushing the coats onto the floor, and curling up on the couch, "Ahhh."

"You guys want to play another game?" Simon seeking his own second wind.

"Enough games, Simon," Becky sits down at the chair once occupied by Kim. "Tuck, you still want to do some cocaine?"

If that's what it takes, "Sure!"

Simon nods his head, "Crazy! How can you keep going?" His eyes pointed at Becky, although the question aimed at both of them. Tuck just shrugged his shoulder, probably barely staying awake.

"You get used to the city life, don't you know?" Becky reached for her purse and started pulling out the instruments.

"Whatever, I'm joining Kim in the other room," Simon stands up and offers his pleasantries, "Good night......" He then saunters into the living room, throws a couple of coats on top of Kim, she only feels comforted and moves just a little, and makes himself a bed on the floor next to the couch. "Night, Kim." She only smiles.

Irvin's decision finally came down to his uncle, Mike Serby. He would understand, whereas Pat would probably hang up the phone and leave him hanging, saying it was his own damn fault. He pushed the numbers and waited for an answer. Three rings, four rings, and the answering machine, "Doggone it! I'm not leaving no message. Who else can I call?" as he hung up the receiver.

"Any answer?" The deputy asked, noticing the hang-up.

"No. I got one more chance," he pushed the numbers, and waited for an answer. Three rings, four rings, five rings, "Come on, answer the phone, please," six rings....

"Hello?"

"Yes, Donna? This is your neighbor, Irvin!"

"Yeah, what do you want?" after squinting to make out the clock radio she had jumped towards the kitchen and picked up the phone as quick as she could. At this hour it had to be an emergency, "What time is it?"

"Say, I don't mean to bother you, but my cows."

"What about your cows? Is this some kind of a prank?" Early morning attitude.

"No, I need your help. I got arrested last night and they won't let me leave."

"Oh. Why did you get arrested?"

"DWI and hitting a deer, I don't know, but can you help me out with the cows?"

"You mean milk the bovines?"

"Yeah, Pete knows how. He's helped me before."

"Well, I can't really say no. How are you going to get back here? When will they let you go?"

83

"I'm not sure, they say I'm still too drunk to drive on my own, but just take care of the cows, please?" Irvin felt he had let enough people down, and the bovines did act as family.

Donna noticed the snow, while gazing out the kitchen window, "Man, Irvin, it might take awhile. It has really snowed!" The snow continued coming down and lay about two feet deep.

"As long as you can get there, please, for the animals sake."

"We'll get there, don't worry. We've got a 'Deere in the shed and, besides, what are neighbors for?"

"Thanks a bunch! I owe you two a lot!"

"Okay, just take care of yourself, and we'll take care of the animals. Bye."

"Good-Bye, Donna," he puts the receiver back into the cradle, a sigh of relief.

"Chop-chop, Tucker boy!" Becky knew she could have been a cheerleader, a model, or an actress, but what the hey. The bottom line was, and still is, she knew how to get what she wanted. "How big you want 'em?" Smiling like a five year old on Christmas morning, after getting everything she had asked for.

"Uh, don't matter. It's your stuff."

"Then I'll make them just right," as she straightened out the two rows, five inches long with a little character. "Just like so."

"All taken care of?" the deputy questioned.

"Yep, my cows are being taken care of," with a little snap to his heels.

"You are a cowboy," as the deputy laid down the paperwork. "Time to go back to your cell, until they get here."

"Oh, they're not coming to get me. I'll just have to wait 'til I'm sober."

"Hugh? But your trucks at the impound."

"Let's just say I have faith."

"Whatever, cowboy. I know I'm not giving you a ride." They walk over to the first locked door, the deputy opens it, and steps to the side, allowing Irvin to go through first.

"Wait a minute!" a voice from behind them, "Is that Irvin Baker?"

"Tis him," the deputy answers.

"Good, I've been waiting for him." Officer Duggan approached the two men and reached out his to Irvin, "I was there last night when we pulled you over."

"Oh," Irvin stands with not much to say. What would he say?

"I need to talk to you in private. Give me all the paperwork on this guy."

"Huh?" the deputy couldn't believe it. "You're not letting him go, are you? The guy's drunk!"

"I'll handle it. Now, give me the paperwork before I have to pull rank on ya." Seniority, public recognition, politics, and a ton of good education had Officer Duggan on top of the County Department, he even ran for mayor a couple of times, succeeding for one term. "Mr. Baker, right this way."

"So, Tuck, you want to go first?" Becky slides the mirror in his direction.

"You go ahead, I'll clean up what's left," ladies first.

Becky picks up the straw and puts herself in ready position.

"Pete! Wake your ugly ass up!" Donna yells and then jumps on top of him.

"Hey, what the...?"

"Come on. We have chores to do!"

"Chores? Your not telling me Baker called us?"

"Yes I am, dear," she gives him a kiss and gets off the bed, taking the covers with her in one sweep.

"Hey! It's cold in here," naked as a Jay-bird.

"Then you best get dressed," no time for nice.

"Oh, you little...."

"Don't say it, I can get worse." Donna could and Pete knew it. "Now come on, I'll make us some quick breakfast."

Pete dragged himself from the bed, taking a glance out the window, "Shit, look at all the snow."

Tuck took his turn at the white line, playing vacuum cleaner with his nose, "Whew, good stuff."

"Only the best. Don't forget your numb," the act of putting a tad on your lip.

84

Tuck smiled, a sort of giggle, reflecting on a story he once heard, "You know what I heard once?"

"What?" Becky tried figuring out the outcome and took a chance, "putting a numb between a girl's legs?" Tuck shook his head, his face turning a bright shade. "Mr. Tuck, is that what you're thinking?"

"Uh, yeah, that's what I heard," Mr. Howdy Doody, himself.

"Well, you can forget about that thought," as she reached over and placed her fingertip on the mirror. She then lifted it to her mouth, and tongued it, "but, do you have another?"

Tuck leaned over to her, looking into her eyes, inviting eyes, "may I kiss you?"

"Mr. Baker, I have some news for you," Duggan walked behind his desk and motioned Irvin to close the door, "please, close it."

Irvin shuts the door and turns about-face, "Good or bad?"

"Take a seat, this might be awhile," a knock at the door. "Come in!"

"You wanted these?" the deputy holds up the folder containing Irvin's record, his history.

"Yeah, thanks," Duggan gets up and reaches for the documents. "Now, make sure no one disturbs us. Unless, of course, you have information concerning Martha Serby." The deputy leaves and the door is closed. Duggan gives a serious eye-check towards Irvin.

"What's with that?" Irvin almost jumps from his seat. "What's with Martha? She's my aunt!"

"That was nice," spoken softly from a beautiful lady, "Tuck, do you want me?"

"Yes, I do," Tuck leans forward and gives her another kiss, a little longer, a little deeper.

"Irvin," Duggan speaks straight, but on the inside it's killing him, "your uncle, Mike Serby, took his life last night."

"Oh, shit! No way! And I'm in here?" Irvin jumps from his chair, "I gotta see him!"

"Irvin, calm down," Duggan comes from behind his desk and offers himself. "I didn't want to tell you in that manner." Irvin falls into his arms. "I'll take you over to the hospital, so you can see him."

"Man," Irvin cries softly, "what else do I have to lose."

"Okay, momma, what's for breakfast?" Pete came around the corner and entered the kitchen, dressed in his warmest—two T-shirts, plaid shirt over them, and corduroys, with thick socks, and don't forget the long underwear. "I'm ready!"

"You goof!" Donna giggled at the sight, herself wearing an extra large sweatshirt and a tight pair of long underwear, "Here, have some eggs and toast. My turn to get dressed." She scooped the eggs from the pan onto a small plate, the toast was already setting in the middle of the table. "You want orange juice or milk?"

He grabbed up and cupped her breast, "Milk, momma!"

"Oh, you," spatula close to the face, "I love you," she bent her head down and delivered an accepting kiss. Pete's hand fell from her breast and came around to grab her butt, pushing her closer.

"Now that you want me," softly whispered, she looks into his eyes, "where do you want me?"

Tuck kept his focus, his eyes fixed on beauty, "wherever you want to go I'll be there." Becky let go from his embrace and stood up. Tuck's eyes never parting.

She holds out her hand, "follow me, my Prince." He stands up, taking her hand, the song begins to play as she leads him down the hallway, second bedroom to the right. ('I've Finally Found The Love Of A Lifetime') Upon entering the bedroom she turns and gives herself to him, embracing with a gentle touch, and searching for his thoughts, "Like a butterfly, I will keep you warm."

"Okay, Irvin, before I take you over to the hospital, do you know where I could locate your uncle's wife, your Aunt Martha?" Duggan spoke unsteady, it was not his best ability telling others about lost family members. "Do you know a telephone number?"

"Yeah," still coming down from the news, hopefully not too far down, "Serby said she stayed in Minneapolis last night with my other aunt, Aunt Kate, Donald and Kate Lannis from Round Park."

"Round Park? Thank you. You don't happen to have a phone number, do you?"

"No. Never thought it much sense carrying those things around," Irvin lightly rubbed his eyes once more, it would be a day of mourning.

Simon had been listening for footprints or laughter, and finally heard soft footsteps. He looked over the couch and watched as Becky led Tuck down the hallway, "I hope he knows what he's doing." Then looking down in front of him he noticed a smile and moved his eyes up to meet a small

85

spark, centered in Kim's eyes. She, too, had been waiting for warmth. With no introduction, no spoken words, he leaned down and gave her a soft kiss, "You are beautiful."

They parted lips, she smiled and combed her fingers through his hair, "and you're a monkey!"

You've been going on a merry ride of life when out of nowhere someone says you're *wrong*! What a cruel thing to tell someone they're wrong. Isn't it?

You start a shouting match and end up not knowing what the argument is about. Or is it just an excuse to cover up your own faults? Einstein gave us an equation for gravity, $E = mc_2$, so, I'll share an equation for getting along.

T(trust) + R(respect) = L(love), and if you don't want to believe it—we all have choices.

"Before I doing any calling let's talk about last night," Duggan caught himself from rushing through his agenda. "First of all I want to hear your story—were you drinking and how much. What were the circumstances?"

Irvin pulled himself together, an expression of suspicion across his face, "You putting me on trial?"

"It's either now or later, kid. If I can get the answers out of you now it might save you from a lot of hassles down the road. Take a seat," Duggan ordered, Irvin obeyed.

Becky and Tuck sat next to each other on the bed, the lights left off, their feelings alert, "Tuck, do you want me?" She takes his hand and places it on her breast.

"Yes," although images of his ex-wife danced in his mind. His hand motionless.

She pulls his hand away and with her other hand undoes the top buttons of her blouse, "Here, I said I would keep you warm," she places his hand back on her breast. He moves his fingers underneath her bra. She reaches out to him, her head stretched towards his, he reacts by meeting her lips with his. He takes his hand from her only to undo the rest of the buttons, she sighs.

The buttons undone he pulls her blouse away from her skirt, she allows him to slip it off, around each shoulder, her skin warm, tender, and soft. Her blouse off she embraces him kissing deeply, her fingernails digging into his back. He tries undoing her bra. She backs away from his kiss, "Troubles?"

"Uh, I can get it," sweating on the inside he keeps trying, his fingers not cooperating.

"Here," she reaches in back of herself and undoes the strap. Tuck's adrenaline rises. She slips off the bra and guides him to lay on the bed. Tuck lays back as she undoes his buttons, pulling his shirt apart and kissing his chest, blowing softly as she directs herself down, further down. His pants become undone by her fingers, her torch inches away from her mouth. She looks up, "Do you need me, Tucker?"

"Oh, yes," a mind full of fireworks, mini-explosions, dizzy dreaming, and wanting nerves. "I want you," he runs his fingers through her hair as his pants come down and he becomes released, "Ohhhh," he tries holding back, his body tense.

Becky teases, her tongue touching, lips kissing, and mouth giving an occasional blow. She engulfs him and scrapes lightly with her teeth on the way back up. She slides her body over him and kisses his chest, his neck, and then to his lips. His hands which formed a tight fist, now push down on her skirt, she wears nothing underneath. She puts her fingertip to his mouth, backing her own lips away, "Are you sure?"

"Ah," a volcano put on hold.

"Maybe we should know each other better. Don't you agree?" she puts her head down on his chest, blowing gently. His body and mind rejected.

Simon had crawled onto the couch. He and Kim now melting into each other, "Simon, are you afraid of love?"

"Sometime," honestly spoken.

She looks into his eyes for insurance, they look back at her, "I feel so comfortable around you."

He rubs his legs softly against hers while hugging and giving small kisses, "You are so beautiful."

The music plays as the light from the dining room creeps into their presence. Keeping each other warm, secure, and needed. Simon stops his legs and his kisses, they each lay on their side facing each other embraced, under a pile of coats, they understand.

"Okay, Irvin," the interrogation had started, "you were at your uncle's bar until closing?"

"Yes, and that's when he came in."

"And you and the bartender sat down with him?"

"Yeah, I didn't even have one drink."

87

"Whatever, the thing I'm mostly concerned with is your uncle's motive," Duggan spoke the truth as he tried to show it, "do you understand?"

Donna came racing into the kitchen, Sampson at her heels, "I'm ready! Let's go get those cows!" Nothing like a big dog jumping for attention. Pete stood up from the table and checked her out while patting Sampson on the head, "Yes, I'll be warm enough." Three layers covered her from the waist up and two layers covered her legs.

"Okay then, let's go. Sampson you stay home."

"You want to smoke one first?" common practice on the weekend.

"Nah, I'm just not into it," Pete thought himself strange, but that's the way he felt, "maybe I've been missing too much church."

Donna delivers a punch to his shoulder, "You Goof!" They share a smile and walk into the small porch where they would slip into their winter gear. "What would my life be without you?" Pete remained silent, not wanting to make a mistake with words, he just grins. Donna notices the unpredictable and shows her dependence, "I'll always have the animals." Burnie still lay asleep at the foot of the bed.

"Irvin," Duggan could see the uneasiness, "would it be better if we tried to get a hold of your aunt?" He tries to work with his suspects.

"Yes! She knows more than I do," Irvin feels relief, the weight off his shoulders. "I don't know what he was thinking." Family secrets are tough to give up.

"Okay, I'll have her number looked up. The name's Lannis, Donald Lannis?" Duggan started to cross the room toward the door.

"Yeah, from Round Lake." Duggan left the room and went to the dispatcher. A phone call would come next.

Martha had been tossing and turning throughout the night, past-flashes, and horror stories, she finally just got up. She took a stroll down the hallway and into the kitchen, "Morning?" Kate is sitting at the table, "Don't you sleep?"

"Mornin' sis, I have my times," Kate offers a grin, "working the night shift sort of messes with your schedule. Know what I mean?" Four years as a Home-Health Aide created it's own habits.

"I guess," Martha faded with the question, being she hadn't worked for the last five years, ever since her youngest had graduated from high school. "Mind if I help myself to the coffee?"

"Go right ahead. What's mine is yours," Kate showed her respect and hospitality, they were some of the picked-up habits. "Still thinking about Mike?"

Martha poured the coffee, waiting for the right answer to come to her, then the phone rang, "Ohh! that startled me..."

Kate stood up from the table and walked to the phone, picking up the receiver, "Lannis residents."

"Yes, this is Officer Duggan, I'm trying to locate Mrs. Martha Serby."

"Um, just hold please," she turns to her sister, "Martha the phones for you."

Tuck managed to lift Becky from his chest, she had fallen asleep, and grabbed some blankets. He threw them over her and then he, too, crawled underneath. "I guess it was meant to happen," he brushed her hair back and gently touched her cheek with his lips, "you're wonderful." He then snuggled up close to her, his mind drifting with warmth and adoration, for both of them.

Donna and Pete managed to get the snowmobile, a reliable John Deere, started after a few pulls, and hit the trail to Irvin's place. The snow had quit falling, but the cows needed immediate attention, and the driveway could wait.

Kate hands the receiver to her sister, "Officer Duggan," and shrugs her shoulders, her face supporting.

"Yes, this is Martha Serby," years working at the high school as a counselor she knows how to hold her composure.

"Mrs. Serby I have your nephew in custody," Duggan starts out slow.

But Martha could sense there was more, "and my husband? What about my husband?" close to breaking, but trying to hold herself. Her sister lays a hand on Martha's shoulder.

"Uh," Duggan did not expect the come-back, "your husband is in the hospital. I'm sorry."

Martha felt somewhat relieved, fearing the worst, "In the hospital? It could be worse, but what did he do?" Martha dug for the truth, the whole truth.

88

"I guess it's a little more than an accident," Duggan is losing this one, no popular votes.

"What is it? Would you just tell me?" Martha's emotions hang on a wire.

"He took his life last night. We were called to his bar around," Duggan now fills in the details.

"I don't care where he did it or when he did it! Where is he now?" her volume going up.

"I'm sorry, but he is in the hospital waiting for proper identification."

"Okay, that's all I ask. I'll be there as soon as I can. Is my nephew going to be there?"

"Yes, just come down to the Hontra police station and I'll release him in your custody."

"Thank you. Tell Irvin Marty's on her way," she puts down the receiver and collapses in her sister's arms, "the fool shot himself, it was in my dream last night."

Pete drove the sled close to the barn, squeezed the accelerator, and made a sharp turn, causing them to tip over, "Hah! Hah!" he laughed in the snowbank.

"You shit!" Donna reacted quickly, jumping to her feet, and throwing snow at Pete. "You could have killed us!"

Pete sat up, still in the snow, "Ah, heck, we weren't gonna get killed, hah, hah."

"Well, come on, we got cows to tend to," she strutted to the barn leaving Pete to pick up the sled.

"I'm sorry, Martha," Kate holds her sister.

"I know, but it's done and there's nothing we can do."

"But pray," another habit she picked up from work.

Duggan walks back into the office and closes the door behind him, "How did she react?" Irvin had been waiting.

"I don't really know," Duggan takes a seat behind the desk, "I don't really know."

"Maybe you've been awake too long."

"Yeah, you could be right. And this is the sort of deal I rather avoid."

"Then why be a cop?"

Duggan stared at the kid across from him, "You know, no one has ever asked me that."

"Uh, before my aunt gets here?" Irvin stays away from the personals, "You mind if I can see Serby on my own? I mean....he's sort of like my dad."

Duggan erases his personal regime, "Yeah, you can do that, and about your DWI?" Irvin's hands squeeze tightly, he prepares for the worst. "According to these files," he pats the folder holding Irvin's records and last night's report, "they messed up when taking your blood test, but I do suggest, and am going to enforce the suggestion that you go to treatment, at least AA."

"Oh, man," the thought of treatment and personal problems.

"Irvin Baker you've been darn lucky in this county and I want to make sure your luck doesn't run out. The deer you hit last night carries a fine by itself."

"Huh?"

"I could make it that way," Duggan gets up from his chair, "so, you want to play games or take care of yourself?"

"Okay, I'll go to treatment."

"And I'll see you tomorrow night at AA, upstairs from the First National Bank. You'll be surprised the people you might know," Duggan reaches out and pats him on the shoulder. "Let's go see your uncle."

Pete had tipped the snowmobile upright and came running into the barn, grabbing Donna from behind, "Baby!" Donna slaps his hand away from her ass and snarls. "You know I love you," he gets into her face, she smiles back. A tender kiss follows.

"I'll wake up Donny. He can drive you back home," Kate parted from her sister.

"Can't you take me?" Martha still reaches out.

Kate shakes her head, a memory of the past lingers in her thoughts, "not since, you know, Alice's death?"

Martha tried to understand, she was the oldest of the three sisters, but she felt as though she knew less, "You can't keep holding on, can you?"

"Marty, Alice and I were very close, and I'm the one who told them to go home that night. They could have easily stayed at a motel!"

"Kate, I'm in the same situation, now! You don't think I stayed awake last night feeling guilty about sending Mike away?" Martha reaches out.

89

"Not yet, sis. It's too hard to go back there. I'll get Donny." Martha is left standing, Kate goes down the hallway to wake up her husband, a stranger in Martha's eyes.

"Giddy-up, cow!" Pete slaps a bovine on the rear, "Get in there," not that the cows needed much coaxing, but Pete just liked to make noises, or was he afraid of the cows.

"Pete, you silly, just leave her alone she'll walk right into her place," Donna, born and raised on a dairy farm, knew the procedure, but she did enjoy the city-boy's reactions. Sure enough, Josie walked right into her stantion. Donna held her arms out, "See?"

"Yeah, now the fun begins," maybe Pete was just playing, wasting time. Go figure.....

Burt woke up to the noise of a snowplow, one of the luxuries being located next to a four-way stop intersection, and now stood in front of the bathroom mirror, "Ah, shit, my head hurts." Trying to dissect last night's events only made his head throb more. He splashes water in his face, grabs a towel, and erases the sleepiness, "Ahh, that's better." He picks up the tube of toothpaste and pushes a small amount onto his fingertip, then rubbing it onto his front teeth. Sticking his mouth under the faucet he fills up with water, and begins to gargle, swish, and slur. He spits out the rinse and nods for accomplishment, he feels clean and fresh. Smiling, he strolls into the living room and notices everything on the floor, "Oh, shit!" One swift kick is delivered to the box and he turns around, headed back to his bedroom, his dream continues.

Officer Duggan opened the front door letting Irvin out first, "Sun's coming out."

"Yep, supposed to be a good day. Compared to last night anything is good." Irvin questioned the comment with his expression, "you wouldn't know, would you?" Duggan asked, somewhat sarcastically.

"Sorry," Irvin shrugged his shoulders not being proud of the black-out.

"Yeah, well, tomorrow night," Duggan held his appointments firm, "I will be seeing you."

"So, do you go to those meetings?"

"We all mistakes and I am not an exception. Come on, you'll hear about it tomorrow." Duggan motioned him to the car, "you can sit in the front."

Kate had woken her husband, Donald, and walked back into the kitchen, "he'll be right out."

"You're sure about this?" Martha asked.

"Yes, and I'm not going to be the one taking you back there. I told you why!"

Martha still finds it hard to take, "you won't take your own sister back to her husband?" The words just came out that way.

"Your husbands dead, Martha!"

"Thank you for clearing the point," Martha's hands went to her face as tears started to flow.

"Oh, I'm sorry," Kate rushes to her side and holds her, "I didn't mean to be so bold."

"Morning ladies, uh, bad timing?" Donald stroked into their presence.

"Do any of these cows have a name?" Donna spoke out of curiosity.

"Oh yeah. Irvin has names for all of 'em, but I can't remember them," Pete thought Irvin somewhat crazy the time he helped him out, naming the cows, talking to them as if they were his brothers and sisters, "yeah, the guy's not all that bad, he just tends to get on my nerves once in a while. Like you do!"

"What! I get on your nerves?" an unexpected comment deserves a small return. Donna picks up a handful of straw and throws it, though it doesn't go nowhere but straight down.

"Now you're throwing things at me?"

"You shit!" Donna jumps into the center aisle and dashes toward Pete. He puts his arms out as if directing traffic to 'stop'. She shakes her head and leaps onto him.

"Ugghh, we're gonna fall!" right against the cow, she doesn't move.

"Now what were saying about me being annoying?" Donna wears a grin with sparkling eyes.

"But, I don't mind it," He grins back and they exchange a kiss. She slides back down to her feet and cups his privates, "Hey, not yet."

"Why not? No one's watching."

"Mooo," enters the language of a cow.

"Excuse me? They're watching," Pete points to the vocal one. "But I tell you what."

Donna sensed a strange commitment, but didn't want to spoil it with her own intuition, "What?"

Pete knelt down on one knee, as if a knight being honored, "Would you...."

90

"Oh, God," Donna gasped.

"Marry me?" He held her hand as he looked into her eyes for an answer.

She knelt down in front of him, rather quickly, falling into his arms, "Yes! Yes I'll marry you!" A chorus of 'Moos' echoed through the barn as a soft light burned between them.

Rainbow's Edge

We have all seen rainbows, if not in the sky, we have experienced them in our own lives, God telling us everything will be all right.

But when we have taken the rainbow for granted and again turned ourselves towards selfishness, competition, and jealousy we put our lives on the edge. Don't play games with Mother Nature and remember, we are here for each other. Enjoy the colors, don't ruin them for the rest of us.

Duggan had second thoughts, "Irvin! How about walking?"

"Huh?" this close to a childhood dream.

"Come on, it's a good morning! The hospital's right down the street, besides, I need to be seen more often." Can you really see the person behind the windows and steering column? Irvin shut the door and followed his message.

"Now, we do have some cows to finish up."

"Yeah, I know, but you're such a sweet-thing," Pete could not resist the miracle in his hands.

Donald walked gently to the coffee-maker and poured himself a cup. Martha softly pushed away from her sister, "You have to quit blaming yourself."

Kate thought she had dropped the subject with an explosion, a detour into Martha's circumstance, "Blame myself for what?" she tried, again, to avoid the pain. Or was it the pain she enjoyed?

"Donald," Martha reached for the third-party, "don't you think Kate should take me home?"

Donald stopped himself from sipping the coffee, "sorry, I don't get involved with family matters."

"So, you just let my sister do whatever she pleases?"

"Wait a minute," Donald sets his cup down, "I take our family very serious, but your family is your business. There is a difference."

"And we, as sisters, are not family?" Martha pushes on for security.

"Once you became married you let go, didn't you?" Donald instructs his theory, "I married your sister, not her family." Martha stands speechless, bows her head. "Now, by the way it looks out there, I have some shoveling to do before anyone can leave."

He walks toward the porchway, "Thank you, Donny," Martha whispers as he walks by her. "I'm sorry Kate." Apologies are accepted.

"So, are we gonna invite these cows to our wedding?" Donna, cheerful.

"We can invite anybody you want, Sweetheart!" Pete hollers back from the other side of the aisle.

"How about my ex-boyfriends?" Hands on hips, a must-know expression.

"Only Simon. He's the only one I'll let in."

"Ha, ha, I love you. You're such a sweetheart." Pete finishes up his job at hand, while Donna escapes into the future, white wardrobe, small church, smiles, and commitment, "Maybe we could have a Christmas wedding."

Pete stands watching her daydream, somehow he heard her whisper, "Anytime, anyplace. It's your dream and I want to be in it."

"You know you are not to blame," Martha approached Kate, "and this time I am not letting a third-party interrupt on something this important.

"Why can't you just leave it alone?" Kate tried backing away, but her feet would not move.

"Because I'm your sister and I care. I want you to be able to enjoy life instead of some accident controlling it." Martha spoke direct, but kept her voice low.

Kate could now pick up her feet and she pushed herself to the cupboard, "Look, Donald never finishes his coffee. What a character."

"Don't slide away, sis. Your life means way too much."

"Then what am I supposed to do, get a divorce?" the unexpected story.

Martha's mouth drops, "Oh, I'm so sorry," she dashes over to Kate and hugs her, "I'm your big sister, lean on me, please." Kate quits the fight and embraces her. "You can come home when you're ready. I love you."

"I love you, too." Donald remains shoveling the snow.

92

Irvin and Officer Duggan approached the hospital, Irvin holding the door open, "Thanks, kid."

"No problem," Irvin stands on shaky ground, "I really don't like these places, hospitals and nursing homes." He enters slowly, his eyes checking out the surroundings.

"How about visiting a dentist or a lawyer? How about standing in front of a judge?" Duggan offered worse places to be. Irvin choked, not wanting to laugh under the circumstances. "Lots worse places to be than this."

"Guess you're right. Where should we go?"

Duggan nodded his head in the appropriate direction, "Right over there, Information desk." Duggan notices Irvin's true persona and takes the lead. Upon reaching the desk Duggan asks for directions, "Can you tell me where I can find Mr. Mike Serby? The ambulance brought him in late last night."

"Let me contact ER." The person behind the desk pushes the necessary buttons and receives the information, "You'll have to take this hallway," the person instructs verbally and physically, "and take the elevator to the basement. A nurse will be waiting for you."

"Thank you, very much," Duggan removes his hat.

"Thank you," the Information Specialist returns with politeness. It's their job.

"Last cow! You want to start scraping the floor?"

"Uh, why don't you scrape the floor and I'll take care of Betsy?"

"Come on, don't be a weenie!"

"All right, but when we get home you're doing the floors." Donna shrugs her shoulder in agreement, at least the kitchen floor wasn't covered with shit, but, then again, Sampson had just moved in a couple of days ago. Pete grabs the scoop shovel and starts to scrape the aisle, thinking about the big dog.

"Okay, ready to go!" Donald enters the kitchen, "I got the driveway cleared for take-off."

"Yes, I'm ready. And sis, remember, whenever you need me I'll be here," she covers her heart with her hand.

"Thank you. Do you want to take any coffee with you?"

"Sure," Donald's feet follow his outstretched arm right off the rug.

"Don't step on my clean floor! What's a matter with you?" Kate repeats the demand for the hundredth time.

"Uh, sorry," an apology repeated for the hundredth time as he cowers into a shell. Martha smiles, it's fun to watch children.

"Hi, you're looking for Mr. Serby?" the nurse asks out of politeness.

"Yes, I'm Officer Duggan and this is Irvin Baker, his nephew."

"I'm sorry," she offers her condolences. Irvin nods with appreciation. "Right down this hallway and to your left. I'll come with you."

"Thanks," Irvin accepted her lead. They walk down the hallway until approaching a set of double doors, "This it?"

"Yes. Just go inside, he'll be laying right in front of you. I will stay out here."

"Me, too," Officer Duggan confirmed. Irvin opens the doors and walks through, his uncle lay on a gurney, the only one in the room.

At first scared, a little nervous, Irvin slowly approaches the covered corpse. Upon reaching the body he takes hold of the sheet and draws it back, uncovering his uncle's face. "Uncle Serb how could you?" His eyes start to melt, he kneels down and takes his uncle's hand, "In God's name, please, be with this man," a weight removes itself from Irvin's shoulders as he continues with the Lord's Prayer and finishes, "Please, Dear God, be with him." Irvin squeezed Serby's hand as tight as he could, the gun he had stolen from his uncle, and had hidden in the alley, would be his own private tombstone for his uncle, a man who died by what he cherished most. "Thank you, God."

Martha and Donald hopped in the car, it had been running for awhile, "I hope my nephew is all right, poor kid."

"Maybe he should have been with you last night."

"Yeah right, Donald. Would you go to a friend of a friend's cousin's wedding?"

"Uh, guess not." This two-hour trip, from Round Lake to Mayville, could become quite a journey.

93

"Does your radio bring in any Christian stations?" Martha pushes the power button. "You know it is Sunday and we should all be in church."

"I'm okay," Irvin states his emotion upon exiting the double doors, "and so is he, Uncle Serb." A grin crosses his face as a tear can't help itself from falling. It's time to walk on.

"I'm sure your aunt will appreciate what you've done. You're a good man, Irvin Baker."

"Thanks," as he turned to meet Duggan's eyes.

"Okay Pete, we're all done! Let's go home and ......" her motions said it all. The cows were let back outside, the skies were clear, the temperature is even raising. "You big stud."

Pete loves the nicknames, "No problem. We're out of here." Pete dashes out of the barn with Donna in pursuit. He reaches the sled and starts pulling the cord, to get it started. She tackles him from the side. They both laugh in the snow, kisses and folly begin to melt the snow even more.

Martha found a radio station suitable for her desire (insert Christian music or music from your favorite artist). Her way of telling Donald to keep his mouth out of her family's business. She could always bring up the word Kate had thrown at her earlier, divorce, but she knew her sister could handle it.

"Thank you for letting me see him," Irvin offers his good-bye to the nurse.

"It's okay. Everything will turn out just fine. We'll do the best to accommodate you and your family in any way. Just keep in contact with us. Good-bye," she offers her hand. Irvin accepts and they hold each other, shaking hands.

"Are we gonna listen to this all the way to Mayville?" Donald Rotten, a spoiled little thing from who-knows-where, whining down the road.

"Yes! And I suggest you listen to the words." Martha Goodness, brought up in a strict home full of discipline and gospel.

Irvin holds the door open for Duggan. The officer steps out into the sunlight and stops, he directs his attention to a church steeple about two blocks away, you can see it through the clearing of tree tops. He hopes Irvin will stop and notice.

Irvin follows the actions of Duggan, he notices the steeple. The bells begin to ring for morning service, "Check it out!" Irvin glows, "It's a rainbow! I never seen one in March."

"They appear all the time, you just have to want to see them." Duggan walks forward as Irvin takes in the ringing and the rainbow, feeling as light as a feather, somewhat high.

Simon awakes, still embraced with a heavenly body. His mind focuses on a futuristic scene, Kim and Simon jogging playfully along the beach, a perfect sky. A knock at the door and Simon's brought back to reality. He gets up from the couch very gently so as not to disturb the sleeping beauty and slides to the front door. It's the guy from last night, "What's he want?" Simon opens the door halfway.

"Morning to you!" A cheery man with a shovel in his hand.

"Yeah, morning to you, too," a somber man who had his dream intruded upon.

"Sorry if I disrupted anything but I've been shoveling around the neighborhood and wondered if you would mind?" He lifts up the shovel.

"Let me check with the owner. I'll be right back," Simon shut the door to just a crack and trotted to the back bedroom where Pat rested. "Pat, someone's at the door," a loud whisper, not wanting to disturb anyone else. "Pat is it all right if this guy shovels your sidewalk?" She remains silent. "Okay, I'll tell him myself." Simon trots back to the front door, opens it, and all he sees is a shovel, "Now wait a minute...." He scratches his head as he scans the landscape, the guy, "I think his name is Bob," is nowhere in sight.

Simon shuts the door and directs his feet to his shoes, then to his coat. He opens the door back up and grabs the shovel. Shutting the door behind him he walks to the end of the sidewalk and takes his first scoop of snow. Upon letting go he notices in the sky—a rainbow. All he can do is smile.

The Poem

Words do not always come easy and when we leave it up to someone else to tell our story it seems to lose its persona. We are all different. We speak in different languages, high voices and low voices. Can we trust someone else to carry out our message?

Yes, for a true friend will do anything for his neighbor, his neighbor's family, and even his neighbor's pets. It is honesty bringing us together.

Tuck wakes with a chilled feeling. He first reaches with his fingers and notices no blankets, "Ugh, it's cold in here." He turns to face Becky and notices himself left with no coverings whatsoever, she has rolled herself up in all of the blankets. "Hey, Sweet-thing," he tries waking her by gently shaking her shoulder.

"Morning Brian," spoken lightly with a smile.

"Brian? Where'd you get that from?"

She opens her eyes, "Can't I call you Brian?"

"My name's Tuck," his middle name is Tuck, but his first name is Brian. He was named after his dad, Brian Tuck Jones, and he hated Junior.

"Okay Brian. I'll call you Tuck," her eyes shut as she goes back to sleep.

Tuck looks at the ceiling, "Sorry dad, wherever you are." Tuck hasn't seen or heard from his dad in ten years. The last news he ever received was from his mom right before leaving the military. He just up and left, that was her story, and no one has heard from his since. "Maybe I should call home today?" He lays in silence until Becky stretches her arm out over him, "Hmmm." He gives her a kiss on the forehead and allows her to embrace him (insert your favorite moment, remember the feeling).

"What, huh, mmm..... thought someone was here," Pat checks out her surroundings. "Must've been a dream. Oh, well, might as well get up anyway." She slides from under the blankets and collects herself on the edge of the bed, wiping the sleep from her eyes. Kim remains nestled on the couch, warm and serene.

"Okay, Irvin, guess it's a waiting game now," Duggan opens the office door. "If you want to wait in here or..."

"Yeah, I might as well. Got any coffee?"

Pat makes it to the bathroom, stretches her face, and grabs her toothbrush, "Whew, what a night."

Simon keeps digging his way closer to the front steps, whistling as he works, starting to forget about where the shovel came from. The skies are clear as the snow has begun to melt. Birds join in with Simon's whistling with notes of their own.

"Martha, are you sure we're going to listen to this music all the way to Mayville?" Donald appears as if a small child not getting his way.

Martha caves in, "Well, it is your car." Donald reaches for the radio knob, pauses for a moment, and then pulls his hand back, "What's a matter? You change your mind?"

"Uh, no. Well maybe," Donald's expression carries a question mark.

"Or do you have something to say?" Martha, High School counselor.

"Um," his words not coming easy, "why don't you like me?"

"You're a spoiled rotten asshole and I can't get rid of you. Is that good enough?" Straight from the hip she delivers her grievance.

"What do you mean? I'm not spoiled," Donald whines in a crackling voice.

Martha reaches for the radio knob and pushes it in, the radio is now off. "Time to get serious Donny. What you said back there about not marrying into my family—are you some kind of a god, some kind of a savior for my little sister, or what?"

"Hey, me and Kate have a good thing! We just don't want no one else sticking their nose into it and spoiling it all."

"Or, are you just afraid of losing her—to her family?"

"Martha this conversation is not making any sense! Why would she want to go back to Mayville, small-town, no business, nothing to do? She has it fine right where she's at!"

"Then why did she mention divorce to me?" Straight from the hip comes another bullet.

"When?!"

95

"This morning when you were shoveling snow it just slipped right out of her mouth. Have you two been talking?" Martha digs for the fault line.

"Oh, man," Donald's hit in the side never thinking about a divorce, "I thought we had everything."

"Do you have any kids, yet?" Strike one. "You know she wants kids."

"Uh, we've talked about it, but....."

"But what Donny? You got some problems going on?"

"Hey! This is personnel."

"I've worked with a lot of personnel problems. I'm trying to save your marriage if you'll let me."

"Oh, like some white knight in shining armor you're going to save the day. What about your husband? Where's he?" Denial comes with a price—hurting others.

"He's dead. Surprised I can come to grips with it?" Martha speaks honestly, "I tried, we tried, for years to communicate, but if he was with us right now in this car and you asked him how his kids were doing he wouldn't have a clue."

"So it comes back to kids?"

"Not always. It comes down to the two people who shared the vows, 'through sickness and in health'."

"So now I'm sick? Is that what you're saying?" Donald's voice begins to rise.

"Let me ask you this—Are you a control freak?"

"Hmmph."

"Do you need to have things your way? Do you watch what your wife spends and how she spends her time? Do you share chores around the house—can you do laundry?"

"Oh, come on, laundry? I think it's time for some music," he reaches for the radio knob.

"Suit yourself, but my advice to you is to talk with your wife and let her enjoy her family—all of them. It's when you're capable of giving to others, others will start giving to you. And one more thing," she stops Donald from pushing the power knob, "if you're not going to give her children at least you could give her a cat." She removes her hand, rolls down her window, and takes in a breath of fresh air. "Thank you, God."

Pat strolls down the hallway and takes a left towards the front door, "The paper should be here." She opens the door, startled to see someone on the top step, "What the...!"

"Just me," Simon stands straight revealing his innocence. "Someone brought me this shovel so I decided to use it. Do you mind?"

"Uh, no, go ahead, but there is a snowblower in the garage," Simon gasps, then looks behind him at a job well-done. "Has the paperboy been here?"

"How you know it's a boy?"

"I'm just saying."

"I know," Simon chuckles, then answers her original question, "but no, I haven't seen any paperperson. Sorry."

"Oh, well, should be here in a bit. You want some coffee?"

"Sounds good to me. I'll be right in."

"What you have to do?" Pat noticed the sidewalk was clear of all snow and so was the front steps.

"Make an angel!" Simon jabbed the shovel into the nearest snowbank, ran from the front steps, and dove, back first, into the highest snowbank, at the end of Pat's sidewalk, and started waving his arms up and down, along with his legs going side to side.

"You're a crazy one Simon! We might have to put you away, yet!" She laughs out loud and takes in the sight of a child, no matter what the age.

"Say, Officer Duggan, I never did get my breakfast," Irvin had thought about speaking up earlier, but didn't want to be a bother.

"I'm sorry. Why didn't you speak up?" Duggan reaches forward from his chair and calls for assistance as Irvin shrugs his shoulder.

Simon gets up from his artistic motif with a smile of art all it's own, "Looking good, Miss Conner."

96

Pat doesn't know if he's talking about the angel or commenting on her morning looks, "Hey, there's a car coming!" She backs up into the doorway, holding the door half open. The car pulls over on the opposite side of the street, in front of the park. A big coat with a hood crawls from the backseat.

Simon notices Pat's insecurity and holds himself back from embarrassing her. He turns toward the big coat and accepts the Sunday Newspaper. "Thanks, have a nice day." A small grumble exits from the hood. Simon peeks into the hood, turns back toward the front door with a bewildered expression as his foot slips on a patch of snow. His foot trips up the big coat and they both fall—the big coat on top of Simon. There's laughter in the air. Simon grins, covering up his mouth as if he had the whole thing planned, while the big coat gets up, falls back down, and gets up again. Pat's laughter brings tears to her eyes.

"Sorry Irvin, no more breakfast. Cut off is 7:30 a.m." Duggan puts the receiver back into the cradle. "How about I treat you to McDonald's?"

"Mickey-D's? Fine with me."

The radio station remains the same as when they left. Donald leaves the tuning alone and listens, not only to the beat, but also to the lyrics, and the words spoken in between songs. Martha has rolled her window back up and shares the music, remaining silent so as not to interrupt the lesson. They still have a ways to travel.

The big coat finally gets balanced and heads back to the car. Simon notices the driver is wearing a smile and looks back to Pat, still bent over with tears. He gets up, fakes a small slide, and walks to the front door, paper in hand, "You been looking for this?"

"You are something else," she takes the paper from Simon and invites him in, then strolls toward the kitchen with her head up and a song in her heels. Shoes off at the door and his coat dropped next to them he walks into the kitchen, giving a small sweep with his fingertips to Kim's cheek as he walks by. She remains silent, moving just a twitch.

Martha reaches over and pushes in the radio knob, the power is off, "Were you listening?"

"Yeah, I heard the song, I was even singing along," Donald shows a little pride.

"And do you know what was being said? Or weren't you listening?" Martha interrogates further.

"I heard the song Martha! What else do you want?"

"Communication," spoken smugly. "Is that too much to ask?"

"Huh, what is with you?"

"I'm a woman and I need to be satisfied."

"Hey, I'm married to your sister and I'm not about to start cheating on her, especially with you."

"Thank you, Donny, but you have just failed test number one."

"Test number one? I failed because I wouldn't sleep with you?" Donald's knuckles get a little white from the tight grip he holds on the steering wheel.

"No, stupid, you failed because you're definition of satisfied is that of a pig! I merely want to be satisfied by sharing points of interest."

"Oh, you mean by... talking?" Donald feels himself stretching.

Martha backhands him in the shoulder area, "Duh!! And you're telling me you actually talk with my sister, but yet you don't know how to satisfy her? She used to volunteer in the library. Isn't that where you met her?"

"You hit pretty hard," Donald rubs the hit area just as a dog whimpers away from his mistake.

"And rightly so. Now start listening!" She turns the power of the radio back on (insert Hymn or Christain Rock, maybe a Country song).

"Hope you like your coffee strong," Pat scoops in an extra cup of grounds. "For some reason I feel like I need it."

"Sometimes you do, sometimes you don't," Simon places himself at the kitchen table and grabs the Sunday Newspaper. "Wonder what the 'Variety' section tells us today?"

"Don't know. Do you use cream or sugar?"

"Nope, just plain old coffee. Here it is, 'Today's Quote', "An artist doing something he enjoys is not a true artist" Hmmm. You believe that?" Simon's usually agreeing appetite is somewhat sour on this note. "An artist doing something he enjoys is not a true artist".

97

"I guess they have to work like the rest of us," Pat joins him at the table.

"But don't you like your job?"

"Yeah, but I'm no artist."

"Could anyone else come in there and run it like you do?"

"I don't know," she shrugs her shoulders looking down at the table.

"Honestly, Patricia!" He snaps a demand.

She raises her head, "No! No one can run it like I can. I rule my office and everyone in it, even if they are all lawyers!" A hair-raising experience.

"Thank you for your honesty, Miss Conner. Is my coffee ready?"

"The cups are right up there, help yourself. You want me to be a bitch? I can be the best." Simon leans forward with serious eyes and grabs Pat by the sleeve of her sweatshirt, "Don't even...."

"Laugh? I can't even laugh," they share a little release with laughter.

"I'll take a Number Three, please," Irvin sounds off his order as they walk through the gates of Mickey-D's.

"And you, sir?"

"Same thing. It looks good," Duggan pulls out his wallet and prepares to pay the attendant. "You eat much fast food?" He asks Irvin.

"No. Try to stay away from it. You know, cows of our own, sort of competition I guess."

"You're kidding, right?"

"Well, I do eat at the cafe or at Serby's once in awhile," he catches himself and sees his uncle laying on the gurney. "It sure can be a cold world can't it?"

"Hey, now, you know your uncle's in a good place," Duggan tries to comfort the ill feelings.

"Here's your order and have a nice day," sounding as if spoken from a script. Duggan picks up the food tray and the two men walk to a nearby booth. Irvin grabs the Sunday Newspaper on the way, his main interest being the Sport page.

Pat poured herself a cup of coffee and then disappeared. Simon had poured himself a cup of coffee and sat back down at the table. He sorted through the sections, Variety, Sport, Travel, and then comes the Comic section, "Here it is." Pat walks back into the kitchen with her purse and sits back down. "Ha, ha, ha, did you read this one?"

"Yeah right, I just got in here. You want to smoke one with me?" Pat opens her purse and takes out her baggie of marijuana.

"Where's your coffee?" Simon notices the missing cup.

"Oh, shit, I forgot it in my room," up from the table she springs.

"As if she needs any. Cool, a poetry contest. Maybe I can win this time." Simon spots an ad for a $10,000.00 contest and rips it from the paper. "I got one just waiting for this." He reaches into his back pocket and pulls out his wallet. "Here it is."

"You got it rolled, yet?" Pat struts back into the kitchen holding her cup of java.

"No, I'll pass on the smoke-down. I'm drinking coffee."

"So? What's the difference?"

"Knock, knock pudding head, the difference is like this," Simon holds his arms far apart. "Coffee brings me up while smoking dope brings me down." His arms following his vocal directions.

"Not me. They both pick me up," Pat starts to roll.

"Whatever. But then, what are you getting up for?"

"Okay already, I won't smoke it if it bothers you that much." She picks up the strands of marijuana, tucks it back into her baggie, and jams her baggie into her purse, "Satisfied?"

"Here, you think I can win anything with this poem?" He hands her a small piece of paper containing typewritten literature. "I wrote it awhile back. See if you like it."

She begins to read; He lives a life a life of pleasure, he lives a life to become God's treasure. Not always easy, he talks with a smile, Never will it be 'til he walks your mile. Take Him by your hand for it's open wide, you will soon understand what you feel inside. On a simple coin he removes the dust, On a simple coin 'In God We Trust'. "Not bad, Simon. Not bad at all," she hands the piece of paper back to him. "Can you make me a copy?"

"Satisfaction guaranteed," she had made Simon's day. Nothing better than someone wanting a piece of you, especially a good piece. "You can have this one."

"So you going to be there tomorrow night?" Duggan questioned the sport's reader.

98

Irvin looks up dumbfounded, he was deeply entrenched by the Ohio State box score, among other teams and highlights, from the Big Dance, "Huh?".

"AA. You are going to be there."

"Yeah, I guess, but what about my uncle. Should we have a wake or something?"

"Yes, you should, and if you and your aunt need any help with anything just call me. Here I'll give you my home number," he reaches for a pen and notepad, both in his shirt pocket, and scribbles down the information. He hands it to Irvin, "Anytime."

"Thanks. Are you sure I have to go tomorrow night?" Be it fear, arrogance, or prejudice Irvin rather not join the club.

"It's for your sake not mine, but I can guarantee a better life for those around you."

"What about me?"

"What about you? The way I see it you died last night."

"Hey, that's pretty cold! I'm right here ain't I?"

"Have you changed in the last twelve hours? Are you concerned about your family and friends? How about Miss Patricia Conner, wouldn't you rather be a better man for her sake?"

"How'd you know?"

"Small town, you think you're gonna keep secrets from anybody? Besides, I'll be there because of personal experience not because of my job," Duggan tries to take the paranoia out of the first step.

"What did you do?"

"DWI, just like you. Why do you think I was mayor of this town for only one term?" Melting down with the rest of the people, in this case Irvin, around him.

"You were mayor of Hontra?"

"Yep, at the same time there was some hot-shot kid playing damn good ball over in Mayville, and I want to know what happened to him," straight from the heart.

"Me? You were watching me play buckets?" A smile to die for.

Duggan wiped his mouth and then chucked the napkin onto the food tray, glancing at his watch, "Your aunt should be here anytime, finish up and let's go."

"You sure you don't want any toast?" Pat repeats the question.

"Okay, I'll have a couple of slices and then I'm gonna go see if anyone else needs help shoveling. By the way, do you have any orange juice?"

Martha pushes in the power knob and the radio is off, "We have to pull in right up here."

"Okay. It's been awhile since I've been here," Donald flicks on the blinker and prepares to turn into Mayville, "hope Irvin had a good night's rest." Martha notices his comment and holds it—maybe he has started to listen. She remains quiet and smiles on the inside.

"So when you go shovel snow what am I supposed to do?" Pat pushes for reaction only.

"You have guests make them feel at home, or maybe call your mom. Tell her about all the excitement before she can tell you."

"You know Simon, you're pretty smart," Pat sets down a small plate with toast and a jar of jelly next to it, "My mom made this stuff!"

Irvin and Duggan walk back to the station, "This has been a different kind of morning for me."

"Yeah, not too often does a person get busted, then let off, and then have to go through what you did," Duggan nods toward the hospital. "I'm serious."

Irvin figures everyone has to make a walk now and then, being born and raised on a farm where cows are shipped away to market, cats are a dime a dozen, and the big watchdog has seen his last days, "The way I see it, there's always a funeral. Everyday."

"You're a strong man, Mr. Baker. Now let's take care of the alcohol," Duggan places his hand upon Irvin's shoulder as they keep on walking.

"Here's the Police Station! Might as well park the car," Martha, somewhat excited, somewhat nervous. "I hope we can get out of here right away. I hate cops."

"So do I," Donald finds they have something in common, but Martha will soon change her mind. Donald parks the car and they both exit the small sedan.

"Aunt Marty!" Irvin yells, a short distance from the parked car. "You made it!" Irvin runs to meet her and gives a big squeeze, "I'm so happy you're here."

"What have they done to you?" Martha is in shock, "You've never acted this way before."

99

Irvin parts from her and looks her straight, "It's about time, huh?" Marty pulls him close as welled up tears begin to flow, "I love you, Aunt Marty."

One Hour Later

After breezing through the neighborhood Simon spent about ten minutes with Burt, waking him up and helping him straighten out the living room. They shared a small conversation about last night's mishaps, what ifs and why nots, and then Simon continued on his way. He did leave Burt with a little piece of paper containing some poetry and the thought of calling his best friend—Patricia Conner. Burt would do exactly what Simon had suggested.

From there on, Simon was heard whistling with the birds and chuckling with the squirrels. His feet hopped, skipped, danced, and totally entertained all those who were watching—we should all be so lucky. He dashed down Main Street, arrived at his parked truck, unlocked the door, and jumped inside. There sits a stranger on the passenger seat, "Morning Simon, are you ready to go home?"

The lives of eight people change, two more if you want to count Pete and Donna, during a thirty hour period. Snow might have had a little to do with it, but the events of nature only serve as a backdrop, a warning if you may. Each person, be it Kim, Becky, or Burt, start to see the world in a different light. The light is not dark but it is clear.

On his way out of town Simon dropped a small note off at Becky's car, he knew she would come for it, along with Tuck. That's if he had convinced Tuck enough about this lady's good qualities. We all take chances. He told Tuck to not worry about his whereabouts, no one kidnapped or persuaded me to leave. I have left on my own.

The note told a little about the future and what to expect. Simon wrote about love, giving, receiving, and also about being used and put-down. Be strong and don't fold to the dogs. Be wise and remember to learn from your mistakes. Follow your path not someone else's.

He wrote it out to Tuck but explained it was for everyone. Tuck, I have another note for you at home. Becky wants to see it but Tuck will not give in. They drive back to Patricia's place and discuss the small words, Pat even shares the poem.

Irvin ends up at his aunt's place to help organize a funeral. They call on Officer Duggan and he's there, ready to serve. Burt had called Pat earlier and they remained close friends—he was about to show up for supper and he was cooking.

Donald and Kate talked about children and a possible move to the country. Donna and Pete discussed the possibility of buying the farm from Irvin. They also started on their wedding plans. Sampson and Burnie never felt better.

Tuck never did call his mom but something still bothers him, "What could it be?" He asks Pat for a ride home. They leave after giving cooking instructions to Becky and Kim, just in case. "Something's on my mind and I just can't figure it out."

They tour the country side until they reach the farm site. Luckily Pat owns a four-wheel drive truck for the snow is deep, "Here we are. You want me to wait for you or are you staying?" He heard this once before.

Tuck walks over to the kitchen table and finds a small note, "Must be Simon, but there are no tire tracks." He reads the note: Tuck, I know my leaving comes at a surprise, but the facts are straightened out and your life, though it seems in shambles, is ready to begin. I was going to prepare a Webpage in your name, but then it wouldn't be yours. I do like the name 'Rainbow's Edge'.

I can see the things you have told me, from having three children, a nice house, a good career, and a family. Try again—You have the opportunity to become a role model for three people (a parent of three children) whose names are Pat, Kim, and Becky. Treat them as your own for they need you. One you will share walking down the aisle, another you'll share in giving and being a true artist, and then there's the black sheep to keep you on your toes. You can also be a mentor for another you'll meet tomorrow night, "AA," although he might have already found one, but there's nothing wrong with two. And one more thing, that little bit of frustration biting at your mind—call your ex-wife. She is the best friend you have—let her do the talking this time.

As for me I never existed—I only held your hand.

Just A Stranger

ABOUT THE AUTHOR

Born amongst the plains and rural farming communities of South Central Minnesota, Scott Lance lived one life while always dreaming of another. Searching the clouds as a young man he was often told about his imagination by his father, but work always came first—and last. Now, about the middle.